CW00505997

One Orange for

Christmas

David K. Treadway

Copyright David K. Treadway 2022

All rights are reserved. No part of this publication may be
reproduced, stored, or transmitted in any form, or by any
means, without the prior written permission of the
copyright owner.

Preface

One Orange for Christmas tells a true story in a unique storytelling fashion. Part One introduces us to the struggles of Sara Tessler, a fictitious character, and her family who live in Bellbrook, Ohio. Sara eventually meets our true character Jill Oliver where Part Two of our story begins, and Jill tells her story in her own words

I had the privilege of meeting Jill Oliver at a Boxing Day dinner in Los Gatos, California in 2006. The conversations that took place around the dinner table that December afternoon began a friendship that I continue to cherish. I knew immediately that Jill's story needed to be told. I was honored in 2019 when Jill gave her permission for me to write her story, and it is here that I get to share it with you, the reader.

"Old enough to remember, young enough not to care"

(citation)

Part One: Meet Sara Tessler

Chapter 1

Sara felt like a caged animal. The feeling was appropriate as she sat in the back of the Bellbrook police cruiser staring at the wire cage separating the back seat from the officers in front. She gazed passively at the crisscrossed wire, her eyes going in and out of focus. Hard to focus, she thought that pretty much summed up her life right now.

Sara was 17 years old and had what some of her former friends described as a deteriorating air about her. Her whole life had seemingly deteriorated in her mind. She was unmotivated, angry most of the time with most of the people around her, and she was struggling to maintain a C average at school. She felt defeated, but it hadn't always seemed this way. All of this was a stark contrast to just two years prior when she carried straight A's in every one of her subjects, was head of the cheerleader squad, head of the yearbook committee, captain of the volleyball team.

She was popular among her circle of friends. Sara had a passionate interest in history which was not the norm among others her age. Her dream was to become an archeologist and was prepping for history and archeology to be her major course of study. Like her friends, Sara had her eyes on college, preparing for a promising future, with a goal of conquering the world. Now she struggled just to get up each morning with any motivation to make it through the day. She had alienated most of her friends and had become a genuine challenge for her parents.

As she sat there in the police car, she realized her teeth were clenched so tight that her jaw was starting to hurt. She was angry, but her anger was all directed outward. In her mind it was others who had steered her life off track. She blamed everyone else for the feeling she had of her life spinning out of control in a downward spiral.

Her parents, Paul and Susan Tessler, were your average suburban couple.

They both were college educated, with good careers that had enabled them to have a comfortable lifestyle for themselves and their two children Sara and Robert.

They didn't spoil their children or lavish them with expensive gifts, but they did reward their hard work and achievements. Most parents would be envious of the relationship Paul and Susan had with their children. They nor their children really wanted for anything more. Like Sara, her brother Robert was a good student and an incredible athlete. Robert was tall, broad shouldered and had the look of a quarterback. He was a three-sport letterman as quarterback of the Bellbrook High School varsity football team, starting guard on the varsity basketball team, and a better than average pitcher on the varsity baseball team. More important to Sara was the fact that he was not only her big brother, but he was genuinely like a best friend as well.

Robert could always make Sara laugh but knew when to be serious and give her the little nudge she needed when she wasn't sure what to do. She always knew he was pleased with her because no matter where they were, whether he was right next to her or if he was at the back of the room, he always did the same thing.

She would look around the room and there he would be, the handsome, athletic young man. He would give her a wink, a big smile, and then give her two thumbs up.

Bellbrook is a small community just south of Dayton, Ohio. In the early years it was your typical small town, with one stop light in the center of town, small local grocery store, Black's Carryout, and the small boutique where school kids would buy $1 friendship rings to go steady with their first loves. Annual festivals like the Sugar Maple Festival and Lion's Club Carnival had been going on for decades, bringing the whole community together during the spring and summer months.

As years progressed it had become a great bedroom community to the larger city just to the north. Even so, it was still small enough that a good portion of the people knew each other through school and civic programs. Some of the citizens had lived in Bellbrook for 50 years or more, with some families going back 4 or 5 generations in the general area. Many in fact had either stayed in Bellbrook after graduating from high school or eventually returned after their college years and raised their families.

For many, their own children attended the same schools and even had some of the same teachers their parents had. It was the ideal place to grow up and raise a family.

Sara and Robert were not your typical siblings who fought constantly or did not want to be around each other. They respected and loved each other.

They were both supportive and proud of each other's accomplishments. She looked up to him not only as a big brother but also as a mentor.

As Robert's senior year had begun, and his graduating was becoming more of a reality, Sara was dreading the thought of him going away to college. She would be finishing her sophomore year and would still have two more years left of high school. Two years without her big brother there every day for her to tease, joke around with, and tell her crazy ideas to. She was proud of him though and tried to encourage him about his future and made sure to conceal how anxious and sad she was that he would be going away at the end of the following summer.

It was the beginning of December that year and opening night of the basketball season was upon them.

Robert had just wrapped up his high school football career by leading their team to the Division AA state championship and was named All-State first team quarterback.

Robert had already earned and accepted a full ride, athletic scholarship to Ohio State. He had been courted by more than a dozen top schools and had his pick of anywhere in the country really that he wanted to go. All that was remained this year was basketball, baseball season, and a summer of traveling with a couple of friends before they all started college in the fall.

Sara lined up with the cheerleading squad at the corner of their home court. She was ready to welcome their varsity team as they ran through the large paper banner that displayed their mascot, an eagle surrounded by the schools' colors of purple and gold. The eagle was swooping down and grabbing in its talons their rival team's mascot, a wimpy looking falcon portrayed with feathers flying in all directions and a frightened look on its face.

The band started playing their fight song and Robert came crashing through the banner, leading their team out onto the court for the first game of the season.

By all accounts it promised to be their best season ever. The capacity crowd cheered while Paul and Susan beamed with pride looking down from the bleachers at their son leading his team with their daughter cheering him on. Susan and Paul watched as their son Robert high-fived his kid sister as he ran past her.

Susan clung to Paul's arm and wondered what they had done so right to have been blessed with these two incredible children. She bowed her head right there with all that was going on around them and simply said, "Thank you God."

The teams met at center court, shook hands with each other and the centers faced off for the first jump ball of the season. The Eagles all-state center was first off, his feet and he tipped the ball out to Robert who took two steps, then passed it off to their other guard Scott. He dribbled to his right before executing a perfect bounce pass to one of their forwards who spotted Robert alone at the top of the circle. The forward fired the ball across the court and as Robert caught the perfect pass, he planted his feet and arched a perfect, eighteen-foot three pointer that hit nothing but net. The crowd went wild.

Robert smiled and pointed at the forward who had fed him the pass. A perfect pass and a perfect shot to the start of what promised to be a perfect season.

The Falcons inbounded the ball and the opposing player dribbled up the court about 10 feet and passed it ahead towards one of their guards. Robert saw the pass coming towards the guy he was guarding. He sidestepped, reached his arm across the face of the other player and intercepted the pass. He dribbled around the guy who had inbounded the ball and left the floor for an easy layup. The player he had stolen the pass from came running full speed from behind, then jumped to block the shot. He hit Robert sideways, causing Robert's body to swing to the side and come down at an awkward angle. He landed on the side of his foot and the momentum caused his foot to bend sideways. The opposing player came down on Robert hard, his full 170 pounds on top of Robert and the entire arena heard the snap.

The crowd gasped as the scene unfolded and instantly fell silent. An instant later, the only sound anyone could hear was Robert's blood-curdling scream. The bone above his ankle had literally snapped in two.

With the weight of the other player still coming down on top of him, the force jammed the broken bone up into his knee joint, completely dislocating his knee.

Players from both teams all backed away in initial shock and then several of his teammates rushed to his side as he continued screaming in pain. Robert's dad pushed students and other parents aside, almost stumbling to the bottom of the bleachers.

He ran onto the court reaching his son at almost the same time as the coaches and team doctor. Paul was numb as he stared down at his son. Robert's ankle literally was hanging on by just a tendon, the bone was sticking out from the base of his leg and his knee was turned at an unnatural angle. As blood began to flow out from the open wound where the bone was sticking out, one of the Falcon players turned away and threw up on the court. Paul saw that Robert was already going into shock and saw his son's skin turning pale. He grabbed his son's hand as Robert began to shake uncontrollably. He was staring straight up towards the ceiling, saying over and over, "I'm sorry Dad, I'm sorry Dad".

Susan had made her way down to courtside with the help of two other parents and as she reached Sara who was huddled with the other cheerleaders, Sara turned and fell into her mother's arms crying.

Sara held her daughter, trying hard not to collapse herself. She wanted to rush to her son's side but was held back by the two parents that had helped her down the bleachers. One of the other parents said, "He's in good hands, Susan, let them do their job."

The town's fire and paramedic squad always had a team on hand at most sporting events and two paramedics were already rushing onto the court. Several players knelt together and prayed, while most of the others just stood and stared in disbelief. Sara raised her head from her mother's shoulder and for some reason her eyes stared up at the scoreboard. The time clock read 19:40, and she had a sick feeling in the pit of her stomach at that moment. The game was already over. Not only her brother's game…. but his career as well. Even though she didn't know the extent of Robert's injury, deep down she knew nothing was going to be the same. Life as Sara knew it had all changed.

Changed because of the first 20 seconds of the first basketball game of the season. She felt everything go black, and she fainted into her mother's arms, almost falling to the floor.

A few moments later, Sara came to, and everything was out of focus. All she could hear was the siren as the ambulance carrying her brother pulled away outside. Her dad had left in the ambulance, heading for the hospital clutching Robert's hand in his. Robert was shaking, obviously still in shock. As Paul looked down at his son, a tear ran down his cheek. He knew he had to stay strong for his son, for his family. He realized there could be a long road to recovery for them all, but especially for his son.

Chapter 2

Sara turned her head and looked out the window of the police cruiser watching as the lights and buildings seemed to pass by in slow motion. She wasn't afraid of what her parents would say or do when they reached the house. She wasn't even sure that's where she was being taken. She didn't really care either. In fact, she didn't care about much of anything anymore. She realized once again that her jaw was locked tight, to the point that her teeth were hurting. She tried to relax, letting herself fall back against the seat, and closed her eyes.

Her mind drifted back to the days following her brother's accident. She had tried to stay strong for Robert, even skipping school to spend days at the hospital sitting at his bedside. He had already been told he would never play football or basketball again, not at any competitive level anyway, and would most likely walk with a limp the rest of his life.

To save his foot, his ankle basically had to be fused together, making it impossible to bend at normal angles even while just trying to walk normally.

The surgery took seven hours to repair what the doctors could of his ankle and completely reconstruct his right knee. The doctors had kept him in practically an induced coma for three days, lying still in his hospital bed, drugged with morphine to mask the pain.

Sara sat in Robert's hospital room and watched as her big brother just stared at the wall at the end of his hospital bed. Teammates, teachers, and dozens of classmates had come to visit continually. The room was filled with flowers, plants, and sports related decorations. The one Robert sat staring at the most was an arrangement that had been sent by Ohio State University.

"There were red and white carnations, with a gray ribbon across the front sporting the OSU logo with the phrase "Best Wishes". The only other thing he would ever receive from the university was the letter saying, "It's with sincere regret that we must inform you of the cancellation of the athletic scholarship that was previously granted.

All of us at OSU wish you the very best and hope that you will still consider Ohio State as you pursue your academic career." Sara would try to talk to him or make small jokes.

She would try to tease him like she always did, but he would simply wave her off angrily as if to tell her just to be quiet. Robert spent seven days total in the hospital, returning home to a hospital bed set up in the family living room with a traction device to keep his leg elevated. It was the same living hell he had endured for the last week, just in a different location.

Sara quit the cheerleading squad. She couldn't conjure up the "cheer" and the "pep" required to be on the team. She couldn't even bring herself to watch another basketball game that season. Robert returned to school almost 4 weeks later. He was walking, but with a full leg brace and a cane. As much as his friends and teammates tried to act normal around him,

Robert knew nothing would ever be normal again. His dream of playing for Ohio State was gone. In twenty brief seconds, his life had changed forever. His scholarship having been rescinded, this left him with the most likely scenario of attending the local junior college.

That was if he even wanted to go to college. At this point Robert simply felt like his life was over, so why even think about college or the future. In his mind, there was no future.

Their parents and teammates tried to get Sara and Robert to go to the final basketball game of the season, but neither were interested in going. The team ended with a mediocre season, having never recovered from losing one of their star players. Robert was still battling constant pain, taking more and more pain killers just to make it through the day.

Paul and Susan tried to get him to counseling but he refused. Robert was understandably in a state of depression and his parents watched it grow worse and worse each day.

Susan was on her knees often in prayer for both her children. Sara continued to try and stay strong for her big brother, at least for a while, but her resolve had begun slipping steadily.

Robert loved his sister, but thought he was doing her a favor by pushing her away. He didn't want his tragic life to hold her back. He felt like he was nothing more than a burden to everyone.

The reality, though, was that in doing so, it was making it worse for Sara and his parents.

As spring came, Sara had gotten back somewhat into of her routine.

She stayed on the yearbook committee and at Robert's encouraging she rejoined the varsity volleyball team. Robert told her, "Sis, you are the family star athlete now; make us proud".

Her team had a decent season and she played well but not at the level she had been capable of before. She almost felt guilty that she was able to play the sports she loved while her best friend and brother sat with his cane watching from the bleachers.

With the end of the school year approaching, Robert's depression worsened as he listened to his friends talk about their plans for the summer.

It was especially upsetting when he would hear his friends talk about their excitement for their upcoming fall college season. Eight of his fellow teammates from the football team had gotten scholarships of one type or another, with two of them receiving partial scholarships to Ohio State.

Robert tried to be happy for his friends, but their good fortune only added to the pain and anger building up inside of him.

Chapter 3:

Sara heard two men talking and was snapped back to reality, back to her horrible present. The two officers in the front seat of the police cruiser were talking but she wasn't paying attention to whatever it was they were saying. She felt a pain in her chest and wondered if maybe she would die of a heart attack, right there in the back seat of a police car. She didn't know if she could have a heart attack at that age, but she knew for certain that her heart was broken. Her whole life was broken. Her mind started racing, making her think of people who'd had life flash before their eyes. Memories began racing through her head at a rapid pace. She started shaking, and then she screamed. The officer in the passenger seat yelled for the driver to pull over. He jumped out of the cruiser and opened the back door to make sure Sara was ok. Sara sat silently now. She had simply needed to get that scream out, to vent, and now she sat and just stared towards the front of the car. The officer watched her for a moment, asking her if she was ok. Once he was convinced nothing was really wrong, he returned to the front seat, and they continued. Sara's mind drifted again.

It was the last day of school. Sara struggled but maintained her grades with an A in all but one of her subjects. Her studies had been a distraction from all of her other troubles. Her mom and her friends had tried to get her to sign up for summer cheerleading camp, hoping she would want to get back on the squad at the beginning of her junior year. She kept telling her friends she just couldn't imagine being able to do it, and she ended the school year with no plans at all for the summer.

Sara was feeling like her parents didn't care about her own emotional struggles she was dealing with. Knowing everything that had happened to Robert, and watching his deepening depression, she felt like her parents were pressuring her to be something she wasn't and never expected to be, a big sister to Robert. Somehow, they thought she was supposed to be his encourager and his mentor. Her mother had on several occasions lashed out at her, yelling, and cursing her for not being stronger for Robert.

Hearing the fighting between his mother and Sara only added to Robert's depression. He finally had relented and agreed to go to a counseling.

He even agreed to start at least for a while to take some mild doses of anti-depressants.

Paul and Susan didn't realize that Robert had stockpiled as much of the pain killers as he could and continued to take the pills long after he supposedly didn't need them anymore. Those, combined with the anti-depressants were rapidly taking him down a path that would not end well if he didn't stop.

The school year had ended on a Friday. Susan and Paul were thankful they could be home from work and spend the weekend with both of their children during what they expected to be a rough weekend emotionally for them. The entirety of the ordeal had strained Paul and Susan's relationship as well as the relationships between them and Sara. That Saturday morning Susan walked into the kitchen to begin her routine of making the morning pot of coffee. She froze when she saw the note propped up against the centerpiece of the kitchen table. She felt a lump beginning to grow in her throat, and her heart sank. She somehow knew what it was without even reading it.

She stood there for a moment unable to move her legs and take the remaining steps towards the table.

She was stone-faced as she slowly walked toward the table to pick up the note. It was an 8 x 10 folded piece of plain paper. On the side facing her it simply said, Mom, Dad, and Sara. Her hands began to shake as she slowly opened the note.

"Dear Mom and Dad, I think you know I could not have asked for a better mother and father. You always worked hard to give me everything I needed, encouraged me to succeed, and were always there with a hand on my shoulder when things didn't go exactly as I thought they should. Sara, you have been the best kid sister a brother could ever have. Just to be clear, I only pretended to laugh at your dumb jokes to make you feel good. Just kidding sis. You always made me laugh and did everything you could to always make me feel like I was the smart one. You're the genius of the family but you're still a dork and don't you ever forget it. Dad I am so sorry I let you down. I know how much my scholarship and playing for Ohio State meant to you.

I was looking forward to standing in the huddle and looking over to the stands and seeing you there, proudly wearing that bright red jersey with your number 14 on it. It would really have been something wouldn't it?

"Who knows, after four years and a national championship under our belt, we might even have made the big time. It was not meant to be though and for that I am truly sorry.

Knowing I let you all down is a worse pain than I ever felt from my accident, and no drugs or therapy can take away that pain. Only one thing can, and I know for all of you, it will be easier in the long run. Please forgive me. I love you all, Robert."

Susan screamed at the top of her lungs, *"Nooooooo!"* She just kept saying "No,No,No", over and over as she ran towards Robert's room. She opened the door and stopped. She began to just weep, looking at her son, lying on his bed, looking peaceful and happy for the first time in a long time. When Paul came running up behind her after hearing her scream, she simply handed him the note over her shoulder, and she stood there frozen, standing in the doorway to the bedroom. Robert only read a couple of lines before grabbing his wife by the shoulders, pulling her out of the doorway and forcing himself into the room.

He screamed for her to call 911. Susan remained immobilized, leaning against the door frame.

"No Paul, let him sleep, he's not hurting anymore."
Susan said numbly. She knew in her heart it was too
late for 911. Too late for therapy or counseling. Her
son's pain was gone, but something in the back of her
mind told her that the worst of hers was just beginning.

Chapter 4

Sara was jolted back to the present by an ambulance crossing the intersection in front of the police car, its siren blaring into her ear drums. She hadn't cried in months, lost instead in a vacuum of numbness and emptiness. She felt something hit her arm and looked down to see that a tear had run down her cheek and dropped onto her arm. She stared at the small drop and wondered if that was all she had left. Was that all the real feeling that remained inside her, all summed up in one little tear drop? She could still hear the siren in the distance, and it brought back the memory of the second worst day of her life.

Paul had taken Robert in his arms, shaking him and begging him to open his eyes. He turned again and yelled to Susan, "Call 911!" Susan looked up at Paul and without emotion said, "Yes, of course", and then slowly turned towards the kitchen. She calmly walked to the phone and dialed 911. When the operator answered with the standard, "911, what's your emergency?" Susan flatly said, "It's my son, I think he's in heaven now." Susan laid the phone down on the kitchen counter and walked away.

She didn't even hear the 911 operator peppering her with questions. Paul was trying to revive his son by applying CPR when he saw Susan slowly walk past the door of her son's room. Susan went into their master bedroom, lay down on the bed, pulled the covers up over herself and closed her eyes.

Sara was half asleep still lying in her bed when she thought she heard someone yelling. She opened her eyes and listened, but nothing. She blinked her eyes several times, trying to focus when she heard it again. Someone was yelling. Were her parents really arguing this early in the morning, the first day of summer break? She thought "Was this how the whole summer was going to be?" Didn't they have any respect for what Robert was still going through?

She jumped out of bed, indignant, ready to march into where her parents were arguing and tell them to stop acting like children. As she came down the hall from her bedroom and entered the kitchen, she heard a small voice from somewhere saying, "Miss? Miss? Hello, I need to know what happened."

Sara turned to see the phone laying on the counter and realized that was where the voice was coming from.

She picked up the phone and asked, "Hello?". The voice on the other end said, "I need to know what happened, you said it was your son?" Perplexed, Sara Questioned, "What? Who is this?" "This is the 911 operator do you need an ambulance?" Sara looked around the kitchen, then down the back hallway that led to Robert's bedroom and then on to her parent's room. She heard her dad crying out, "Robert, please come back, please!". Sara, ignoring the 911 dispatcher on the other end as the phone dropped to the floor. She ran down the hall in a panic. When she was almost to the door of Robert's bedroom her eyes fell on a folded piece of paper lying on the floor in the doorway.

She could see the words, "Mom, Dad, and Sara" As she stared at the piece of paper, her mind started putting it together, the note, the yelling, screaming, 911. She raised her head slowly and saw her father practically on top of Robert pressing rhythmically on his chest. She watched her dad, tears streaming down his face, begging his son to come back to him. When she looked towards her brother's face and saw his pale white appearance, she felt her legs go numb and she collapsed to the floor. When she opened her eyes a few minutes later she could hear a siren off in the distance.

As the sound of the siren grew closer, every sound around her seemed to be pressing harder and harder on the sides of her head.

She was jolted back to the present. From the back of the police cruiser Sara suddenly asked one of the officers in front, "Who died?" Officer Tomlinson turned and said, "What do you mean, Sara?" Sara replied, "The ambulance, that siren... who died? It always means someone died."

Officer Tomlinson happened to be the Chief of Police in their small suburban community, and he had known the Tessler's most of his life. Steve Tomlinson and Paul had been college roommates at Ohio State. They remained friends after they both earned their degrees and at Paul's urging, Steve had settled in the same community as Paul and Susan.

He applied to the local police force and had worked his way up through the ranks, becoming the police chief at the beginning of that previous summer.

The Tessler's had introduced Steve to his future wife, a lifelong friend of Susan's. Susan and Steve's wife Connie had been best friends literally since kindergarten.

The Tomlinson's son Erik played with Robert on the high school football and basketball teams. Robert and Erik both had received scholarships to their dads' alma mater, Ohio State. Both families were the modern version of a Norman Rockwell story told through one of his iconic paintings. Small-town families, great kids who excelled in school, both scholastically and athletically, parents with stable good-paying jobs. They were the typical "All-American family". They even had their typical squabbles and disagreements and their occasional arguments from time to time.

Most people would probably be envious of the lives that the Tomlinson's and Tessler's enjoyed. The chief looked in his rearview mirror at Sara staring directly at him through the wire barrier and said, "Sara, that ambulance might be going to save someone."

Sara scoffed out loud but then her voice trailed off as she bitterly responded with, "They didn't save Robert." Steve's heart was breaking for Sara and the only reason he was driving in the direction of Paul and Sara's house instead of the lock-up facility at the station was because of the relationship their families shared. His son Erik had taken Robert's accident hard.

He had taken the death of his friend even harder. To his credit, after mourning his friend's death he was moving on with his life. One of the last things Robert had said to Erik was, "Okay bud, it's up to you to make both of our dads proud." It sounded or felt cliché, but Erik knew that Robert would want nothing less than success for his best friend. He was determined to not only make his dad proud but Robert as well.

Sara assumed they were on their way to the police station, but she noticed a few landmarks they were passing and realized he was taking her to her parents' house. She guessed it didn't really matter at this point. It wasn't as though they weren't going to find out what had happened. She doubted Mr. Tomlinson was just going to drop her off at the end of the driveway and say, "Have a good night, Half-Pint." That had been his nickname for her for as long as she could remember. Even though she knew the answer, she asked him anyway. "Where are we going?" Steve answered, "Not where you should be going, at least not yet anyway."

Sara shrugged her shoulders and apathetically mumbled, "Whatever", and turned away with a look of disgust on her face.

Steve just looked away and slowly shook his head back and forth. He had resolved in his mind to do whatever he could to try and help Paul and Susan not lose their only remaining child.

As far as Sara's parents knew, she was at the mall with a couple of friends. These were friends that Paul and Susan were not thrilled to have their daughter hanging around with, but they had tried hard to be supportive in any way they could. They were trying to just let her go through this grieving process, hoping that eventually she would return to her old self. In the months since Robert's accident Sara had gradually alienated most of her previous friends. Sara's cheerleading friends and volleyball friends all tried to keep things the way they had always been, but the harder they all tried, the angrier Sara got, and she eventually pushed them all away.

Sara's regular group of friends had undergone a troublesome change as Sara began spending time with different girls at school, which bothered Paul and Susan. She had started hanging out with what some of the other students referred to as, "the misfits", since they all seemed to just not fit in.

Most would probably consider them your typical rebellious teenagers who, in their striving to be different, ended up horribly successful in their efforts. It wasn't so much the multiple piercings - the more unusual the placement on their body, the better in their opinion. It wasn't the way the misfits all chose to dress in their different way. They didn't all dress in black or paint their faces pasty-white or choose a particular stark hair die, they were in-fact all different even among themselves. That was another reason for the name "Misfits" the other students had given them. The real title referred to the group's anger towards everyone and everything. One girl did however embrace the whole grunge look. She was the one that Sara was most drawn to because she seemed the most withdrawn. In truth that is what Sara wanted for herself, she wanted to just withdraw. She had even wondered to herself several times if Robert was the brave one by doing what he did. Sara was in a dangerous place and didn't realize it.

Chapter: 5

Paul and Susan were both sitting in the living room of their home with Susan working a crossword puzzle, while Paul was writing a report for work. Susan was the first to notice the reflection of car lights shining through the living room window, which meant someone was pulling into their driveway. Susan got up and walked over to the window. She couldn't see inside the car, but she clearly made out it was one of the local police cruisers.

Her husband heard the concern in her voice as she called his name. When she saw their friend and Chief of Police, Steve as he got out of his car, Paul heard Susan murmur, "Oh God, please, no, please". Paul rushed to the window and saw Steve approaching their front door. Susan was already heading there to answer it. She swung the door open at almost the same time Steve reached the front step. Susan's voice broke as she said, "Is it Sara, please tell me she...". Steve held up his hand to interrupt her from saying anything more. He quickly assured her saying, "Sara is alright, she's not hurt". Susan felt her shoulders drop.

She drew in a deep breath as relief washed over her that Sara wasn't hurt, or worse. She paused to catch her breath.

At about that moment, Paul reached the open door and motioned for Steve to come inside. "What's up with the surprise visit Steve, and in the cruiser at this time of evening?" You said Sara isn't hurt, but is she with you? Or what is going on?" Steve held up his hand to stop Paul and said, "Can we sit down?" That made Susan nervous again as they led Steve to one of the chairs as Paul and Susan sat on the sofa, with Steve across from them.

After Steve had left the cruiser for her house, Sara asked in a sarcastic tone to officer Dixon, the other officer still sitting in the front, "So what now?" Dixon had a teen-aged daughter of his own. He had been wondering how this evening would be different, had it been him receiving the visit and not Paul and Susan, and what he would be thinking. What if he was the one sitting in that house right now having to listen to his friend and police chief talk about the events of the evening involving his daughter? Dixon didn't look back at Sara.

He shook his head and simply said, "I don't know." His mind was still preoccupied thinking about his own daughter. They sat down in the living room and Steve said, "I have Sara out in the cruiser." Susan stared back at Steve with a puzzled look. Paul looked at his friend with his eyebrows raised.

His look was one that understood that whatever was coming next wasn't going to be totally pleasant. At least from what Steve had said though, Sara wasn't hurt, and Paul was relieved about that. Steve continued, "Sara is in a little trouble. Hopefully we can keep it from turning into big trouble, but it's serious."

Susan interrupted him and started to stand saying, "Can I go see her? Why didn't you bring her in the house?" Paul placed his arm on Susan's and gently pulled her back down on the sofa, saying, "I think we should let Steve finish what he has to say." Susan sat back down and put her hand on top of Paul's that still rested on her arm when he had pulled her back to sit. Steve continued, "One of my officers answered a call about something suspicious down at the museum across from the park."

Susan and Paul saw the troubled look on Steve's face as he struggled to share the details of what had taken place.

Chapter 6:

The museum was one block up from the center of town, a four-way stop that still had what was once the only stop light in town. The original town limits had only stretched the distance of about 4 or 5 blocks in each direction from that main intersection. The town charter dated back to 1816, just over 10 years after the entire county was officially founded. The museum sat across from the park, housed in one of the original old homes of the early community. Part of the home was actually the log cabin that dated back to the early 1800's and had been added on in the later years to make it a fairly large four- bedroom, two story dwelling. The entire house still dated back to the mid-1800's and had been preserved when the 4th-generation owner, Mrs. Berryhill, had donated both the house, and the small lot it sat on to the town, with the stipulation that it be used and maintained as a town museum.

The town of Bellbrook had some artifacts stored in one of the township office storage rooms, but there had never had a place to adequately display them. There was a rich and diverse history here, but it had remained just a small town 12 miles south of Dayton.

Dayton was one of the larger and better-known cities of Ohio. Bellbrook had several families in the area whose ancestors dated back to the towns founding. It had expanded over the years, growing quite a bit just in the last few decades.

Now, the stored artifacts finally had a place to call home, and over the years people, had donated various items to the museum that had some significance to the town's history. Occasionally the museum would host a collection highlighting a specific time in the history of the area, or a particular event, family, or cultural theme with items on loan from various residents.

As the police cruiser had continued down the highway, on the way to her house, Sara thought back to what had taken place just thirty minutes earlier. She was with her four friends, the misfits. They had been walking around the side streets and back alleyways of Bellbrook. One of the girls always seemed to be leading the pack, and all five of the girls were feeling especially angry this night. They often talked with each other about how their parents argued all the time, and a couple of the girls shared far worse things about their parents.

Janie who liked to wear old ragged looking men's clothing had a very abusive father. Stephanie had an alcoholic mother who started her drinking about nine o'clock in the morning and continued the rest of the day. Debbie had been shuffled around foster homes most of her younger years. That girl's experience basically amounted to a life where the foster parents took in kids just for the money and nothing else. She felt used by adults. Georgia was the oldest and just as angry at everything as the rest of the girls. Sara was angry for different reasons though. Her parents argued more than she remembered them ever doing so before. The stress of everything that had happened does that to couples she supposed but that didn't make her feel sorry for them. She wasn't in an abusive home, but like the rest of the girls, she was still extremely angry at her parents and others. Like the other girls, she basically hated her life. She really hated those who kept telling her, "It's going to be okay." She wanted to slap the next person that said that, because in her mind, nothing was ever going to be okay again.

The girls were about a block from the center of town when one of the girls pointed to the Bellbrook Historical Museum building.

She said, "What a stupid waste of time. That old building is one of my parent's passions. They spend hours volunteering there for things.

I guess dead things or dead people are more important to them than..." She paused and turned towards the other girls and said, "Hey ladies, you want to have some fun?" The girls shrugged their shoulders and one said, "I'm always game for some fun." Janie said, "Come on, follow me."

She led them down a side street and ducked under an old chain link fence. Sara looked up and realized they were in the back yard of the museum. The girl leading them said to no one in particular, "Let's show them what's really important."

They approached the back of the building, where were concrete stairs led up to the back door. The girl leading the rest stepped up to the top landing and tried the doorknob. Another one of the girls, Georgia, giggled and said, "What are you doing?" The other girl turned and looking at the other girls proposed, "Ladies, let's go have a history lesson." She had pulled the sleeve of her sweatshirt down over her hand.

She looked back at the other girls then punched the glass in the lower left corner, the pane closest to the doorknob. The glass cracked and she pushed her hand through, shattering the glass the rest of the way. Pieces fell on the landing at her feet and inside the closed door.

The girls looked around wondering if the sound of the breaking glass had caught anyone's attention. They waited to see if any lights came on from nearby buildings or homes. When the girl was sure they were in the clear, she reached to inside the broken window and toward the side, then unlocked the deadbolt and the doorknob. When she turned the inside knob, the door creaked open.

The girls made their way into the back of the building. It was almost completely dark with only a small amount of light coming in from surrounding streetlights through various windows. One of the girls took out her cell phone and turned on the flashlight feature. The other girls followed suit. One of the girls said to the girl who had broken the glass on the door, "So what do you have in mind Janie?"

Before answering the other girl, her eyes narrowed as an evil looking smile came across her face.

She was thinking of what she could do most to hurt her parents. She turned to the girl who had asked her the question, "I'm going to teach my parents a lesson. Come on help me." The girl took out a red magic marker that she always carried in her pocket. As they entered one of the main rooms towards the front of the building, the girls all waved their lights around, taking in the time capsule of items displayed on the walls. There were antique photographs in ornate frames and what looked like ancient kitchen utensils neatly hung. On the floor there were pieces of furniture placed neatly around the room, books on shelves, along with other items.

Sara had a momentary flashback to her studies in history, and the passion those stories held for her. The stories when she imagined what was behind a particular old piece of furniture and where it had come from or who had made it. She would see a book and wonder who had held it and how they had acquired it. She often would think further back to things of ancient history. She was about to say, "We can't be here; let's go", when she was snapped out of her thoughts by the lead girl who declared, "Well, well, well, my loving mother loaned that to the museum just last month. She was so proud." Then she screamed out, "You witch!"

The girl's eyes had fallen on an old antique baby carriage with a vintage- looking doll sitting up in the carriage. She walked over and grabbed the doll out of the carriage, then started twisting the dolls head. She twisted and pulled until finally the doll's head broke from the rest of the body. She threw both pieces back into the carriage.

She looked down at the broken doll saying bitterly, "Well mommy dearest, I guess the little girl you loved more than me isn't so beautiful anymore, is she?" The girls all came over and looked down into the baby carriage and watched as the one who had torn the dolls head off, mumbled something under her breath and then spit on the headless doll.

Another girl, Georgia caught on to what the girl was doing. She remarked, "Yeah, my mom has her favorite little things she spends way more time with than she ever thought about spending with me. She's into all this antique crap too." The words of the two girls whipped the other girls into a bit of a frenzy. One of the girls took a marker of her own out of her pocket, walked over to an old oak bench and wrote across the top of the backrest, *"Just a stupid piece of wood."*

The other girls started looking around the room for something to vandalize, to vent their anger against.

As Sara walked around the room shining her light on different artifacts, her light suddenly fell on a display of old trophies that must have been on loan from the high school. Her eyes fell on one of the trophies.

It was a basketball trophy. It said something about district champions or something. She didn't even take time to read the whole inscription. Her anger flared inside her. She said to herself, "Basketball ruined my life, it ruined my family. It killed my…" Her voice and thoughts trailed off and then Sara gritted her teeth as she picked up the trophy. She turned and in front of her sat a beautiful antique buffet. She raised the trophy over her head, clinched her jaw, and smashed the gold cup of the trophy down onto the front of the buffet. The cup didn't break off, but the force of the blow bent it at an awkward angle. She swung it down again harder this time.

The cup broke the rest of the way off from the base and clattered to the floor. A large chunk of wood from the buffet was left splintered, hanging down the front of the once beautiful piece of furniture.

Sara let a smile form on her lips, a smile that quickly changed to a snarled look of anger.

An instant later, all the girls froze when they heard someone yell, "Police! Who's ever in here, come out with your hands raised." None of the girls made a sound. They all immediately turned off the lights on their cell phones. They could see the light from a flashlight scanning around the next room. As the officer entered the room where the girls stood motionless, one of them shoved him from the side.

He fell against a piece of furniture, catching his wrist between two slats of a rocking chair. As he tried to regain his balance one of the girls picked up a small metal oil lamp and threw it towards the officer. She wasn't really trying to hit him but wanted to distract him further so they could escape out the back door where they had come in.

The lamp struck the officer in the forehead causing him to stumble over a rocking chair. His wrist, trapped between the slats in the rocking chair, bent at a sideways angle and he fell as he heard and felt his wrist crack. He screamed out in pain and then yelled to his partner, "Terry, help!"

As the girls ran through the doorway trying to escape, they came face-to-face with the other officer.

Terry had his gun drawn and a flashlight shining in their faces. The officer yelled, "Police! Down on the ground, NOW!" The girls froze again. There was no place to go now. The first officer had regained his footing, he was bleeding from his forehead and his wrist was throbbing in pain. He looked around the room and found a light switch, so he flicked it on. The second officer, Terry exclaimed, "What the hell! What are you girls doing?" He looked at his partner who had blood running down the side of his forehead and he yelled at the girls, "Lay face down, hands behind your heads!" One by one, he handcuffed the girls and told them to stay down. He reached for his radio and called the station, requesting back up and an ambulance, officer injured."

Paul rubbed his forehead and let out a deep breath saying, "Ok Steve, just tell us. What did Sara do?" "Sara and some other girls are in some trouble, possibly some big trouble depending on how a few things unfold next." Steve said. Susan had a quizzical look on her face as she interrupted the police chief.

"But Sara was at the mall, what happened there?" Paul placed his other free hand on his wife's, "Let's let him finish."

Steve continued. "Sara and her friends broke into the town museum. After they broke in, they vandalized the place." Susan couldn't help but stop him there, protesting, "No, that can't be! Sara wouldn't do something like that!" As she said it, she knew what she had just said was not true. The truth was that she didn't actually know what her daughter was capable of doing. She shook her head back and forth as Steve went on. "They broke a few items, wrote things on the walls and on some of the antique furniture. Given more time they might have caused more significant damage. Fortunately, someone passing by had noticed lights moving around inside the museum. Apparently, the kids were using the flashlight feature on their cell phones.

"It was their cellphones that the passerby noticed, I guess. That's when the 911 call came in that something suspicious might be going on in the museum building." Susan interrupted him again and said in a thoughtful tone, "Of course we will help pay for any damage and trust me, Sara will work to pay for every penny of it."

Steve cut her off, saying in a more serious tone, "It's not that simple Susan. He drew in another deep breath before saying, "One of my officers was assaulted". Paul and Susan's eyes both opened wide.

Susan put her hand to her mouth. Steve continued, "He possibly has a broken wrist and probably will have several stitches for a pretty deep cut on his forehead. He is on his way to the hospital up on Wilmington Pike right now. We still need to sort things out and I am not sure yet which of the kids caused the injuries to the officer, technically though, just like with any crime, they are all considered accomplices to anything that took place. I will do what I can, but Sara could be looking at charges of trespassing, breaking, and entering, vandalism, attempted robbery, and worst of all, assaulting a police officer."

Susan pulled her arm away from Paul's hand and buried her face in both of her hands and started to cry. Paul dropped his head down, staring at the floor. He sucked in a hard breath in an effort not to break down in front of his wife and his friend, but he felt defeated just the same. He wrapped both arms tightly around his wife and pulled her close to him.

Everything that had happened in the last year and a half had taken its toll. He had tried his best to be the strong one for his wife and daughter. He felt now like he had failed miserably. He had his moments after Robert's accident when he would be alone and would fight back the tears in a losing battle. Several times while standing in the garage he would lash out and punch whatever was nearby with his fist. After Robert died, he had tried to keep most of those moments private because he knew breaking down in front of Susan and Sara would only cause them more pain.

Paul stood up and took a few steps away from where they all had been sitting together. He wasn't really walking anywhere in particular, he simply took a few steps and then turned to walk back, saying to Steve, "Steve, can I go talk to her?" Steve said, "I'm sorry Paul, I can't let you do that, not right now anyway. The other kids are already on their way to the station with some of my other officers. I thought I owed it to you and Susan to come by here first, and let you know what was going on. But first I need to take Sara down to the station now for questioning just like the other kids. She hasn't been officially placed under arrest, but she will be.

"You are welcome to follow me down to the station, but I can't let you see or talk to Sara yet and you will need to wait in the front lobby of the station. We need to get things sorted out. They are all juveniles except one possibly and that at least is one thing in their favor if even that can be considered a positive in this whole situation. Paul, Susan, I'm sorry."

Chapter 7

As Steve rose from his seat, he turned towards Paul
and put his hand on Paul's shoulder. "You can follow
me down to the station and we'll see if we can get this
all sorted out." "Do you think we should call our
attorney?" Paul asked. "That might be a good idea"
Steve answered. Susan's mind was racing, and she was
trying to concentrate but all she could think about at
that moment was Robert and the drastic turn their lives
had taken in such a short time. She ran to grab her
purse while Paul was pulling the car out of the garage.
She didn't even remember to lock the front door. She
was practically in a trance, and she was feeling a heavy
pressure on her chest. She even thought that she might
be having a heart attack. What she did know for sure
was that her heart was breaking at that moment. It was
breaking for Robert and for Sara. It was breaking for
all that Paul had gone through. She thought about how
strong he had been during the last year and a half since
that fateful night at the basketball game. She wondered
how much longer they both could keep their own sanity.
How much longer could they hang on to what they had
left as a family?

As she climbed into the car Paul was already on his cell phone calling their attorney and friend, Sam Retherford. As they pulled away from the house and down their street, Paul gave Sam the small bit of information he knew, and Sam told him he would meet them down at the police station. When he disconnected from the call Susan as much to herself as to Paul said, "What are we going to do?" Paul simply said, "Pray sweetheart, right now, just pray."

It was only a few miles to downtown where the police station was. Paul noticed another couple getting out of a car in the parking lot and rightly assumed they were parents of one of the other girls involved in the incident at the museum. As they entered the police station, Steve was waiting in the lobby as they entered the police station. The chief asked them and the other couple to have a seat and he would be right with them. Steve and another officer had taken Sara into one of the small rooms down the hall they used for questioning witnesses and suspects. All the girls involved had been kept separate and each had been read the required Miranda rights after they were formally arrested. The only difference was they were juveniles. They had the right to have their parents present, along with an attorney.

Paul and Susan didn't really know the kids Sara had started hanging out with, so in turn they didn't know their parents. This was much different from the way they knew the parents of the kids that were involved in sports and other school activities that their son and daughter had participated in. They could only assume these parents were good people, good people, just struggling with their own kids. Struggling to understand, and like Paul and Susan, struggling to try and fix it. Whatever "it" happened to be in this case. Susan looked over at the other couple sitting opposite of them. She saw the same look on the woman's face that she felt. Susan decided to reach out to the other woman. "I'm Susan and this is my husband, Paul." Paul stood up and offered his hand. The woman forced a half smile and shook his hand. The other man reached and shook Paul's hand as well. Paul sat back down and said, "I assume you guys are here for the same reason we are, your child is in one of those rooms down the hall because of the museum break-in?"

The man nodded his head up and down, then said apologetically, "I'm sorry, my name is Dan, and this is my wife, Julie." Paul and Susan shook their heads, acknowledging the introduction.

Julie with a scared and confused look on her face blurted out, "Our Janie isn't a bad girl." Susan got up and went over to sit down next to Julie. She put her arm around Julie's shoulders. "I'm sure she is Julie. Hey! We will all get through this." Dan looked at Susan and silently mouthed the words, "Thank you" to Susan. Dan and Julie had no doubt just experienced the same shock and anxiety that Susan and Paul were going through. Susan had surprised herself, pulling it together and now serving as a comforter to another hurting mom.

Paul said helpfully, "Dan and Julie, our friend and attorney Sam Retherford is on his way. If there is anything we can do to help, we surely will. I am sure Mr. Retherford will be willing to help also if you need anything." Paul gave a nervous laugh and said, "I guess we don't have to imagine what you are both going through right now. So seriously if we can help." Julie and her husband at the same time said, "Thank you."

The four sat in silence for a bit. They could all hear muffled talking coming from different areas of the police station, the occasional door slamming closed, and phones ringing. Susan for some reason was transfixed on the sound of a typewriter coming from an open door.

The sound was coming from down the hall. It was a welcome distraction, as brief as it was.

Dan was the first to speak again. "We've had trouble with Janie, but nothing this serious. Nothing involving any type of criminal act. We've never been through anything like this. We don't even have an attorney because we've never needed one for anything, so we appreciate the offer to introduce us to your friend, I mean your attorney." Paul said, "Absolutely, don't worry about it." He added with a slight smile, "And he's not only our attorney but he is a friend as well. He's a good guy and even more important right now, he's a good attorney."

Julie turned to Susan, saying, "Susan, can I ask you something?" "Of course." Susan replied. Julie kind of looked away for a moment and then turned back and looked at Susan. "Our Janie really is a good kid. We've had some things happen in our family, and then Janie started to change. I can't blame it on the other kids she hangs out with. That would be too easy I guess or maybe a lazy excuse. My question though is: Is it my fault? I don't know what your situation is with, I'm sorry I don't even know if it's your son or daughter."

Paul interrupted saying, "It's our daughter Sara." Julie was trying to hold back her tears and her next question surprised Susan, but she immediately understood Julie's meaning and was not offended by it.

As tears started to roll down Julie's cheeks she asked, "Do you blame yourself like I do?" Dan in a scolding tone said, "Julie!" Paul held up his hand towards Dan, saying, "No, it's ok." Paul knew in a strange way that they were all kindred spirits at that moment, so anything that was said could maybe help all of them deal with what was going on.

Julie's question might have seemed odd if it were not for the fact that both Paul and Susan at times had done exactly that, blame themselves. Susan knew the other woman was hurting and did not take her question in the wrong way. She knew some of the same pain. Susan thought about her question for a moment. She had gone through those same emotions and questions over and over for months now.

Was she to blame for everything that had happened to their family? Was there anything she could have done differently? Was it really her fault that Robert had chosen to take his own life?

Susan glanced over at Paul and then turned back to Julie. She began to speak. "You know Julie, I've asked myself that same thing. What could I have done different?" Susan was holding back her own tears but continued.

"I've asked myself whether it was something I did to make our Sara hurt so much that she's changed in the way that she has. We also had some things happen with our family and I know deep down none of it was my fault. I still question though how I could have done and said things differently to help Sara. Maybe at some point I'll think of some things, but the truth is, right now, I don't know." One side of Dan's lips turned up in a half-hearted smile and said, "We really appreciate your openness. I really don't know what we're going to do. You know, you do all the things you think you are supposed to do. You work hard, to provide, you at least think you are going out of your way to teach your kids about living a good life, and most of all to hopefully not make the same mistakes you made, no matter how small or silly those mistakes might have been.

You love your kids, and you want the best for them. But then when things go off script, wow!

"You look at yourself in the mirror and you ask, what did I do wrong?"

Paul gave a nervous laugh under his breath before saying, "So Dan, how did you get inside my head to know all the things I've felt too?" Both men traded half smiles with each other. Susan remarked, "You know I believe fate brings people together for a reason. Let's all try our best to get through whatever is going on right now. Maybe then we can help each other." With a look of relief on her face, Julie choked back more tears. She looked directly at Susan saying, "Thank you so much Susan. I've shared my thoughts with Dan, and he's been great, but I've never felt like he could possibly understand what I'm going through. I realize now I can't understand his feelings and emotions totally either."

Chapter 8

Police Chief Steve genuinely cared about all four of the kids, but because of his relationship with Paul and Susan, he wanted to make sure he was the one to question Sara. As he entered the room where she sat it looked as though maybe the gravity of the situation had begun to set in for her. She had lost that look of "I couldn't care less" and now just looked like a scared little girl. That didn't mean she didn't still have an attitude and she quickly recovered her darker demeanor when she snapped at Steve, "Just leave me alone. And by the way, you didn't read me my rights." In a stern tone Steve told her, "Leaving you alone is not an option."

Then Steve leaned over the edge of the table towards Sara and waited until she looked up at him. "Look Sara, I don't have to read you your rights until you are officially placed under arrest, which as you might have guessed, has already happened to your friends in the other room. I'm not your parent and right now I'm not your friend, I'm the Chief of Police and, young lady you are in a lot of trouble. You can sit there and act like you don't care. You can even say that you don't give a rip.

"Maybe you don't. I'll tell you this though, you had better start caring. Your parents are sitting out in the lobby right now probably wondering if they are about to lose their only other child, and I'm wondering that myself. I will not just sit back and let it happen." Steve raised his voice a little more, "You got that?"

Steve's look and seriousness in his voice had taken Sara's bravado down a couple of notches and she almost politely answered him with, "Yes Sir." Steve's next words took her by surprise. "Sara put your hands out in front of you." Sara looked up at him kind of confused but did as she was told. When her hands were out in front of her Steve leaned over the table and placed handcuffs on her wrist while saying, "Sara Tessler, you are under arrest, you have the right to remain silent, if you give up that right, anything you say can and will be used against you in a court of law. You have the right to an attorney and to have the attorney present during any questioning. If you cannot afford an attorney, one will be provided for you. Do you understand these rights?" Sara's eyes were opened a little wider now and she looked genuinely scared. She looked silently at Police Chief Steve for a moment.

"Can I talk to my parents?" Sara finally said. Steve maintained his serious cop demeanor. Without answering Sara's question, he repeated in a little louder tone, "Sara, do you understand the rights I have just read to you?" Sara sat back in her seat a little and stared at the wall in front of her and said in a soft tone, "Yes". "I can't hear you." Steve responded sternly. Sara again answered, "Yes." a little bit louder.

More for effect but also to allow himself to take a few deep breaths and compose himself, Steve left the room without saying another word. He hoped his parting words and the ensuing silence would get through to Sara just how serious her situation was.

Steve went out into the lobby and walked over to Paul and Susan motioning for them to follow him into the hallway. When the door had closed behind them Steve turned to them saying, "I haven't really questioned her at all. All I have done is try to get across to her how serious her situation is right now. Here's where we are. Just like with an adult, she's been read her rights. I formally placed her under arrest and that is when I read her the Miranda rights. That statement made Susan realize again the seriousness of it all.

The police chief continued, "She has the right to have an attorney present before answering any questions and since she is a minor, she has the right to have her parents present before and while an attorney is present. Like I said at the house, I'm going to try everything I can to help her. This is much more serious on account of the officer being assaulted and injured. It's no longer just a case of breaking and entering and vandalism. When we enter the room, I would ask that you both stay calm, don't raise your voice, and just let me ask the questions. You guys okay with that?" Paul and Susan both simply nodded.

Steve softened his tone, as he told them, "Just a heads-up, to try and make her understand how serious the situation is, when I told her she was under arrest I had her put her hands out and I put handcuffs on her. So, don't freak out when you see that. As your friend and not as the Chief of Police, can I pray with you before we go talk to Sara?" Susan said appreciatively, "Oh Steve absolutely, and thank you." Steve placed a hand upon a shoulder of each of his longtime friends and bowed his head.

"Dear heavenly Father, right now we ask for your guidance and wisdom. We ask for your comfort for Paul and Susan. Give them a peace, your peace Lord that surpasses all understanding. We lift Sara to you Father God and ask that you would break that hardness that is in her heart right now. Even as we speak, I pray that she would begin to look to you for strength. Help us all through this time Lord God. Please give Susan and Paul patience and wisdom. Help us that we would do and say the right things. Lord, touch Sara's heart right now. In your precious name we pray, Amen." Susan looked up at Steve with tears in her eyes. "Thank you, Steve, thank you." Paul took in a deep breath and said to no one in particular, "Okay, let's do this."

Chapter 9

As the three of them entered the room, Sara looked up, and when she saw her parents, she lowered her head, and they could all hear her let out a hard breath. Whether it was anger at seeing them, or frustration or something else, they weren't sure. Maybe it was in part the realization that things were getting real now. When Susan saw her daughter handcuffed, she felt angry, then she just stared down at the cuffs on her daughter's wrists. Strangely her next thought was, *"That's supposed to be a corsage around her wrist for her senior prom."* She felt a pain in her chest and knew that another little piece of her heart was breaking again. She wasn't sure how many pieces were left at this point.

Steve motioned towards the chairs on the opposite side of the table, facing Sara. "Let's have a seat. Paul and Susan, as the police chief now I need to tell you that I have formally placed Sara under arrest, and I have read the Miranda rights to her. Now Sara, I want to make sure you understand, with your parents present, did you understand your rights that were read to you that you can have an attorney and your parents present before answering any questions?" Sara nodded.

"Sara, I need a verbal yes or no.", Steve said. Sara looked up at Steve then over at her parents and as she turned her head back to the chief, rolling her eyes, said in a sarcastic tone, "Yes." Sara's dad said sternly, "That's Yes Sir' Sara." Steve held up his hand towards Paul to remind him that he'd asked them to stay calm and let him do the talking. Sara did as her dad had insisted though and in an even tone answered, "Yes sir". It was all Paul and Susan could do to stay quiet and not pepper their daughter with questions. They honored Steve's request though and let him do the talking.

Steve calmly asked, "Sara, do you mind telling me what happened tonight?" Sara's words surprised them as she exclaimed, "I don't have to tell you anything, do I." Her words sounded like more of a statement than a question, but surprisingly, without any kind of attitude. Steve responded, "No Sara you don't have to say anything if you don't want to, but it would be helpful if you cooperated right now. Like I said earlier, this is very serious, and any cooperation you give me now could only help your situation in the long run." He paused for a moment and then continued, "One of the officers who responded to the break-in at the museum was assaulted.

"Sara, even if you weren't the one that assaulted him, you were present, and by all accounts you were involved in that break-in. So typically, for anyone involved in a crime, what one person commits, all are held responsible. So, it could help your cause if you answered some questions, especially if you were not the one involved in what happened to that officer. By the way, that officer is currently at the hospital getting stitches in his forehead, and x-rays on his injured wrist, which very well could be broken. So, this is serious Sara." There was a knock on the door and a uniformed officer stuck his head in and said, "Sir, a Mr. Retherford is here. He says he is the Tessler's attorney. The chief looked over at Paul and Susan and motioned with his head towards the door to let them know to follow him out.

They all shook hands with Sam Retherford. He was actually friends with all three of them. It was one of the advantages or curses of living in a small town, everyone knows everyone. Steve explained the situation to Sam, emphasizing the injuries to his officer. He told Sam he had read Sara her rights and had asked if she would answer any questions. He told them that she had not done so up to that point.

Sam asked if it was alright if he, Paul and Susan spoke with Sara privately for a few minutes and Steve agreed with, "Okay Sam, let's all work together to try and save this kid." Susan drew in a hard breath when she heard that statement, 'save this kid.' At that moment, Susan had the image in her mind of her son's grave. Paul sensed her reaction and put his arm around her shoulder and drew her close to him. Steve opened the door to the interview room saying, "Sara, your parents and Mr. Retherford can have a few minutes alone with you." He stepped back allowing the three of them to go into the room. Steve shut the door behind him, leaving the four of them alone.

Paul pulled an extra chair from the corner of the room so that all three of them could sit down. Susan for the first time took a look around the very plain looking room, and then down at Sara with the cuffs on her wrists. Sara was staring forward not really looking any one of them in the eye. Sam spoke first, "Sara, can you tell me what happened tonight?

"I really need to know the exact details, who did what and especially what happened with the officer that was injured."

To try and defuse the situation a little Paul said very calmly, "Sara, if you will let us, we'll work through this together. I want you to look at me Sara." Sara looked up at her dad as he continued. "Sara, we are all still struggling with everything that has happened in the last year and a half or so, and we are all dealing with it in different ways. I say that only so that you might understand that I can't feel the same exact things you are feeling. Like I said, we are all dealing with it in different ways. As a parent, I have different emotions and feelings about what happened than you would as a sister. What I do know though, and I want you to really think about this, the path you are on, is this what Robert would want for you?"

Sara's lower lip began to quiver, for the second time that night, a tear rolled down her cheek. She jerked her head towards her father and almost yelled, "How would you know what Robert would have wanted? You might as well have stuffed all those pills down his throat just to get rid of him."

Sara felt like she was on the verge of breaking down, but she fought the urge to just let go and start crying.

Paul was stunned by his daughter's words and felt defeated at that moment.

His thoughts came back that had gone through his head so many times, questioning if there was anything else he could have done to save his son. He looked away from his daughter and dropped his head slowly to stare at the table. Susan snapped at Sara saying, "Sara, that is not fair, and you know it." Paul reached over and put his hand on his wife's arm and shaking his head said in response, "It's okay honey." Paul got up and walked towards the door.

He motioned to Sam who followed him out. Paul looked at his friend the police chief, and asked, "Is it ok for you to take the cuffs off? I think it will help her to calm down enough now to talk to us." Steve nodded his approval and came back into the room saying, "Sara I am removing the handcuffs, but you are still under arrest. Do you understand?" Sara nodded that she understood. Neither Steve nor Paul made an issue of her not verbally answering the chief. Steve removed the cuffs, then turned and walked towards the door. He turned back and said to all of them, "I really shouldn't do this.

"I'll give you guys a few more minutes alone with her."
He left the room, closing the door behind him.

Susan reached across the table and took one of
Sara's hands in hers. She said, "Sara, how about you
tell us what happened." Sara lowered her head and
closed her eyes, and then took in a deep breath. She
looked up but not directly at any of the three adults
across the table from her.

She began, "Me and some friends were just out
messing around, hanging out downtown. One of the
girls really hates her parents." Sara paused there and
looked sideways at her own parents and continued, "she
told us her mom and dad were really involved in the
museum. She wanted to do something to hurt them. So,
we followed her to the back of the building. She put her
hand under her shirt and punched her fist into the pane
of glass and broke it. Then she reached through the
window and unlocked the door from inside and we all
went in. She kind of went crazy and started turning
over pieces of furniture and took out a magic marker
and started making marks on different things. We all
kind of got caught up in what she was doing. I didn't
damage anything, I didn't."

She lowered her voice then and said, "At least I don't remember. I think I turned over a chair and pushed some things off a shelf. I don't really remember everything.

"A few minutes later, we heard someone yell something from the back room and we all froze. A police officer walked into the room and yelled *"Police! nobody move"*, or something like that. I really don't remember much after that. That's pretty much it. Eventually more officers arrived including Mr. Tomlinson, I mean Police Chief Tomlinson, and he had one of his officers put me in his car and I assumed they took the others in different cars. That's all. I didn't touch that officer or hurt him. I didn't."

Paul and Sam walked out of the room without commenting. Sam agreed to tell Steve exactly what Sara had told them in hopes he would work with the district attorney to go easy on Sara. Nothing else could be done until in the morning when the judge could release Sara and the others either with bond or simply released into the custody of their parents. Susan asked Steve to please let her take Sara home. Paul had disagreed.

"Maybe sitting in a holding cell for the rest of the night might really let this all sink in for her." Paul said.

One by one, the other girls involved, Stephanie, Janie, Georgia, and Debbie had pretty much corroborated Sara's recounting of the events of the evening. The girl who pushed the officer admitted doing so. The girl who threw the lamp confessed she had been the one that had thrown it. She also confirmed which girl it was that pushed the officer, causing his injuries. That at least was something in Sara's favor.

Shortly after 9:00 the next morning, Steve called Paul and Susan to let them know the judge had agreed to release Sara into their custody and that she would have to appear in court in a couple of days.

The ride home from the police station was quiet. Sara thought about how her life had changed so drastically in such a short period of time. To a teenager though, a year or two can seem like an eternity. She closed her eyes and for what seemed like the thousandth time, she saw her brother steal that pass and sprint towards the basket. She was bolted back to the present when she felt the car come to a stop. She had the same thought she had so many times.

She wondered where she would be right now if Robert hadn't stolen that pass in the first 20 seconds of that stupid basketball game. The words of her father came to her mind, "Is this what Robert would want for you?" She felt ashamed, but still was filled with anger over the horrible hand that life had dealt her, her brother, and her parents. She wondered what would come next. Would she have to spend some time in a juvenile detention center or camp of some kind, she thought to herself as she looked out the car window and watched the world go by.

All she wanted right now was to sleep, but she was expecting a long lecture when they got home. To her surprise, when they entered the house, Paul said, "Sara, go on to your room. I'm sure you need some rest. When you get back up, then we'll figure out what is next." Sara started towards her room and thought it best to not turn back to look at her parents. Paul and Susan watched her until she disappeared into the hallway at the top of the stairs.

Paul turned and took his wife into his arms and just held her for a long time.

Susan started to say something, but Paul gently put two fingers to her lips and softly told her, "Shhhhh, Let's go fix some breakfast.

Chapter 10

Sara fell into a deep sleep almost the minute her head hit the pillow. The nightmares that had plagued her so many times in the last year or so came back with a vengence. She found herself running from something. Like in all the previous dreams, She was dirty and sweaty, and her pajamas were tattered and torn.

She would look back, not seeing anything or anyone, but she knew something was pursuing her and she was trying desperately to get away from whatever it was. In her previous dreams the scenario was the same, but with every episode it seemed as though whatever was chasing her was coming closer than her previous nightmares. She felt that if it ever caught her, she would surely die. She was always on the brink of total exhaustion, ready to collapse on the damp ground of the woods she was running through, but then she would wake up. It was as though she was watching a horror movie, only she was the main character that was destined to die a horrible death at the end. This time though, even in her deep state of sleep, she could tell something was different. She wasn't waking up this time.

She thought to herself, why was this time different? What was coming next? She was running as hard as she could. She dared to steal a glance back to see if she could see what was chasing her. When she turned forward to see where she was going, her head smacked into a low-hanging tree limb. She fell hard to the ground and lay there, daze, stunned by the blow. Something warm was trickling down her cheek, and she felt it with her fingers. She pulled them away and saw blood.

As she tried to get up again, she realized she couldn't move. It was if she had been paralyzed by the fall. As she lay there unable to feel her arms or legs, the sound she heard was much scarier. Instead of the sound of someone running hard behind her, and tree limbs cracking from whatever it was chasing her, the woods had gone silent. She thought maybe she had woken up and was back in her bed.

As she stared up, though, she saw the trees blowing in the wind, and the moon dancing back and forth between the leaves as the limbs swayed in the trees. Then suddenly a twig snapped. The sound though, came after the long pause of silence.

She thought to herself that whatever it was, it had found its prey and was taking its time before finishing it off. The sound was coming from the direction she had run from.

She strained, trying to see, but she couldn't move her head to look back. Then she heard the sound again, only this time something had changed. She tried to focus, and there it was, the crushing leaves and snapping of twigs. Confused, she realized this time it was coming from in front of her. She realized though; the sounds were also still coming from behind her. Gasping for breath, she cried out loud, "Oh God, please!"

She was in that state of a dream where her subconscious knew she was dreaming, and if she if she could just wake up, it would be over. She tried to scream to wake herself up, but no sound came out. The footsteps grew louder. Hard footsteps coming closer, more leaves crushing, limbs breaking, and those low, menacing growling sounds. The wind suddenly started blowing the limbs in the trees above her more fiercely, whipping them to back and forth violently. The branches resembled long skeletal fingers. She could only move her eyes back and forth.

She was straining to see what was coming closer with each of the steps she heard. The sounds were still coming from both directions. She could hear the footsteps only a few feet away now, but she still could not move. Then suddenly the footsteps stopped. The lump in her throat seemed to block her airway, and she realized she wasn't breathing. She was trying to gasp for air, trying to scream, but nothing. All at once, something grabbed both of her feet and began to drag her over the ground. Then something or someone grabbed both of her hands and pulled them backwards above her head and tried pulling her body in the opposite direction.

It was as if two creatures were engaged in a violent tug-of-war with her body. She felt her arms stretched to the limit and thought they would literally be pulled out from their sockets, and her legs felt like they might even separate from her hips. The pain was like nothing she had ever felt. She thought, "Is this how I am going to die? In my sleep, in a nightmare, literally being pulled apart?" As her body continued being pulled in both directions, rain began to fall.

Within seconds it became a torrential downpour. Still being unable to move, and gasping for air while trying to scream, the rain began filling her nostrils and her mouth. Desperation and fear added to the agony of the physical pain from being pulled apart. Now, as her mouth filled with water, she felt like she was drowning. She wanted it to be over. She thought, "just let me die, and all the pain will go away." She was resigned to the thought that she was going to die that night.

As the thought of wanting to die ran through her mind, both creatures suddenly let out a blood-curdling shriek as they seemed to pull even harder. She was lifted off the ground, stretched between two unseen forces that were fighting to take her. The creatures both shrieked and howled as she felt one last yank from each before, they let go of her hands and feet. She closed her eyes, and it seemed like she was suspended in midair for several seconds as she thought, "Did they let me go, or did they actually rip my arms and legs from my body?" As the creatures both howled again, her body dropped. She didn't hit the ground, but still felt herself falling. It felt like everything was moving in slow motion. As she fell, she heard violent footsteps from all directions now, but she was confused.

She couldn't tell if they were running toward her or away from her. A crack of lightning jolted her out of her dream and into full consciousness. She could hear pouring rain outside, and it confirmed that she was awake. She was covered in sweat and was shaking. She lay there for a long time, afraid to go back to sleep. Almost an hour went by before she felt herself finally drift back to sleep.

Chapter 11

Paul and Susan spent the next day praying for their daughter and for God to help give them guidance. They felt like they were on the verge of losing their only remaining child. Susan wept, pleading for God to heal Sara's pain and bring her back to them whole again. Paul held Susan in his arms, trying to comfort her as she continued to cry. Paul felt numb and found himself simply repeating, "Please, please, please." That was the only thing that came to his mind, literally pleading as Susan was for their daughter's life - the life they felt was slipping away.

They let Sara sleep most of the day. About 4:00 that afternoon, Susan went to her room and knocked. She heard a faint "yes" and opened the door. Sara was sitting on her bed staring out the window. She wasn't really focusing on anything, just staring. Susan simply watched her daughter for a moment before speaking, then asked if she was hungry. The only response from Sara was a silent shake of her head to say no. Susan said, "I'm going to bring you up something and if you want to eat it a little later, that's ok." Later in the evening, Paul and Susan decided to go to Sara's room.

When they went in, they could see she had eaten a little bit of the food Susan had brought earlier. They both thought that was a good sign. Sara was holding something in her hand, but Paul and Susan couldn't see what it was. When they had entered, they saw her hand drop to her side as though she wanted to hide whatever she was holding. "Sara, what do you have in your hand?" Susan said. Sara didn't acknowledge her mother or look at either of her parents. Showing a little frustration in his voice, Paul said, "Sara, your mother asked you a question." Sarcastically Sara said, "I thought I had the right to remain silent?" Paul pointed a finger in Sara's direction, ready to say something scolding to put her in her place. Before he could speak, Susan touched his arm and he paused. Paul looked at his wife, and she shook her head back and forth. Susan whispered, "Let's wait." They turned without saying anything more, then left and closed the door behind them.

Sara looked back to make sure they were gone. She lifted her hand that held the object she had hidden to her side. It was a small frame that held several pictures of herself and her brother Robert.

They were making crazy faces in different poses at one of those photo booths at the mall. Sara remembered the day vividly.

It was one of those days when she had been struggling with some things and Robert took her to the mall for some ice cream and just to hang out. She just stared at it. She remembered how Robert's favorite thing to call her was a dork. She always knew he was just joking and was never offended. The second picture in the frame showed Robert looking like he was making a fish face, and she remembered he was saying, "Doooork" as the camera had flashed. She gave a little laugh under her breath. It was the first time she had felt like laughing or even smiling in a long time. That only made her mad at herself. She didn't want to laugh or be happy.

Even though it scared her, she welcomed the pain. She felt she deserved to be in pain. She wanted the pain to consume her whole being at that moment. She looked at the third picture in the frame. Robert was winking and giving two thumbs up like he always did to say to her, "Hey, everything is going to be okay."

It seemed off in the distance, but she heard herself saying over and over, "Why, why, why?" She felt a rage come over her. As the anger grew, she drew her arm back to hurl the framed photos across the room. It didn't break, but it bounced off the wall and landed face-down on the floor. She just stared down at it with disgust in her eyes. She felt disgust towards her parents, towards school, and most of all towards Robert for not still being there for her.

Chapter 12:

Paul and Susan were hoping they would hear from the court by the next morning so they would at least see an end to this interminable wait. Susan thought maybe, if they could hear whatever was going to happen next, then they could figure out the right words to use with their daughter.

The next morning, they did hear from the court and were told that Sara needed to come into the court at 1:00 PM that afternoon. They called Sam, their attorney right away and he assured them he would be there. Susan went to Sara's room and knocked. She waited a few seconds and opened the door. Sara was laying on her back, staring up at the ceiling. Susan told her that they had to get to the court at 1:00 that afternoon, and for her to please be cleaned up and ready on time.

Paul and Susan waited until an hour before they were all supposed to be at court, and they still had not heard Sara up and getting ready. Susan went to Sara's bedroom and knocked. She waited a moment and then knocked once more, but still heard no response. She knocked louder and called out firmly, "Sara!", but still nothing.

Susan felt the same sinking feeling she had experienced when she opened the door to Robert's bedroom that morning that seemed like ages ago. She slowly opened the door, fearing the worst. She was met with sudden feelings of relief and confusion at the same time. Sara was not in her room. Susan had just passed by the hall bathroom and knew Sara wasn't in there because that door was open. She walked over and opened the closet door because that was the only other place her daughter could be.

From downstairs, Paul had heard when Susan raised her voice and knocking louder on a door. Frantically he came running up the stairs. Susan turned to Paul and simply said, "She's not here." Paul said, "What do you mean she's not here?" Paul hurried into the room, looking for where she might be. His first thought was, "Thank God, there's no note." In some ways that was a relief, since he found his mind going back to that darkest day of their life.

Paul and Susan went to every room in the house, calling out Sara's name as they covered the entire home. Susan searched all through the garage while Paul looked in the back yard... still no Sara.

Susan told Paul that both cars were still in the driveway, so she knew Sara hadn't driven off anywhere.

"She must have gone for a walk or something. We're supposed to be at the court in an hour, she can't afford to be late." Paul said. Susan grabbed her husband's arm and said, "Let's take both cars and go opposite directions. Maybe she is just walking around the block."

They backed the cars out of the garage, and both left down the street in their own direction. As they both came around to their own street again, they pulled up next to each other, both shaking their heads in dismay. Neither had seen Sara. "I'm going to drive towards the high school; maybe she walked over there." Susan said. Paul was already moving his car forward as he said, "Okay, I'll keep looking other places." Neither of them was as concerned about being late for the court appearance as they were in finding Sara safe and sound. They knew the state of mind Sara had been in the last year, and it was anybody's guess where her mind was after the events of the previous evening. There was no telling what she might be thinking, or what she might do. Susan tried to block those thoughts from her mind.

Her only focus right now was to find Sara. She drove the familiar route towards the high school, looking down the side streets as she drove. She almost ran up along the curb, distracted as she looked to the left and right. Fortunately, there were no parked cars, or she would have run into the back of one that may have been parked along the side of the street.

Paul didn't really know where Sara's new friends lived, so he couldn't go by their homes. The only thing he thought of was perhaps trying a couple of places where her old friends' homes were. The friends she no longer hung out with. As he drove, he prayed. He realized he was gripping the steering wheel so tightly that his knuckles had grown white. He felt his hands shaking as he clung to the steering wheel. He tried to relax but he continued to feel the anxiety trying to take over. "Pull it together," he told himself out loud. Like Susan, he looked down the side streets as he drove, hoping to spot Sara simply walking down the sidewalk of one of the random streets.

So far, neither of them had seen anything other than the normal neighborhood activities. They saw a few kids out throwing a ball or playing street hockey.

Several people were out doing their exercise walks, and a couple of joggers. As Paul passed one street, about halfway down the block he saw a girl walking.

He slammed on the brakes and quickly backed up. As he turned and proceeded down the street, he slowed the car as he got closer to the girl walking. The girl heard the car approaching from behind and looked back nervously, wondering why this car was slowing down. Paul saw the girl's face and realized that it wasn't Sara. He groaned aloud, showing his frustration. He could see that the girl was looking at him strangely. He thought to himself, "Oh good grief, I probably scared the girl half to death." He rolled the passenger window down and yelled out, "I'm so sorry, I didn't mean to frighten you, I am looking for my daughter Sara." The girl nodded slowly, maintaining a suspicious look on her face. She turned to the right and hurried up the next driveway. Paul thought, "Great, now I'm going to get pulled over and questioned for stalking a teenaged girl in my car." He shook his head in exasperation.

It was then that Paul suddenly had an idea of where Sara might have gone.

He quickly made his way around the block and back to the main road. As he reached the center of town and the original four-way stop light, it was red from his direction. He began talking to the red light, saying, "Come on, come on, come on." It seemed like an eternity before it changed green allowing him to make the left turn onto Upper Bellbrook Rd. He prayed his hunch was right about where she might be. He drove over the top of the hill and down. He put his right turn signal on and turned slowly into the Bellbrook Cemetery. If she was there, he didn't want to startle her and have her take off running into the wooded area that bordered the back or left side of the cemetery.

He parked in the center roadway that cut across the middle of the cemetery. As he got out of the car, he looked about 50 yards away. Sure enough, there was Sara sitting on the concrete bench they had placed in front of Robert's grave.

Chapter 13:

Paul slowly approached, again not wanting to startle Sara. When he was about 20 feet away, he could hear her crying. He stood next to a tree, listening, his heart breaking for his daughter. Then he heard her start to speak. "Robbie, I never thought I could hate you, but right now I hate you. I hate you more than I have ever hated anything or anyone." She let out a long, anguished sob, and started again.

"I hate you for leaving me Robbie. You were my best friend and the one I depended on. I could come to you easier than going to Mom and Dad with a problem. You took that away from me and I hate you for that. I hate you for what you did to our family. Mom and Dad have never been the same. I have never been the same. Look at me now Robbie, is this what you wanted?" She raised her voice and yelled, "IS IT?" Sara began sobbing again, and Paul took a couple of steps towards her, but when he heard her start up again, he paused. "What am I supposed to do now, Robbie? You remember when I broke up with my first boyfriend? You passed by my bedroom and heard me crying. You quietly came in and sat down next to me.

"You put your arm around me. When I looked up at you with tears running down both cheeks, you said, "What's wrong, Dork?" All I could do is laugh through my tears at that moment and that took away a little of the pain I was feeling. You had that gift, Robbie. You could calm whatever storm I was going through with just a couple of words, or a little joke or jab at me like we always would do to each other. You would make me laugh and I would forget what was making me hurt at that moment.

When I told you that Kenny and I had broken up, do you remember what you said? You said, "Hey Dork, didn't you know he was gay?" That made me laugh again, and I buried my head into your shoulder, and you hugged me tighter. You just held me and let me have my cry. Then you said what always seemed to fix everything. You said, "I think we need to go to the Dairy Shed, Dork and get a big Chocolate Sundae." And that's what we did. As we sat outside eating our ice cream. I remember I stopped mid-bite and looked at you and said, "Is Kenny really gay?" You shrugged your shoulders and said, "Oh, I don't know. What makes you think that?" I just laughed and shook my head. I didn't cry over Kenny any more after that."

She began sobbing again, and slowly stood up and walked towards Robert's headstone. She knelt in front of the grave marker and started pounding her fist on top of the granite, screaming, "*I hate you*! I hate you because I'm still suffering, and you aren't." She stood and backed up a few feet, and then bent down to pick up a small rock and threw it at the gravestone, yelling "Are you listening? Do you hear me? I said *I HATE YOU!*"

She walked slowly again towards Robert's grave. She dropped to her knees and sobbed as she put her arms on top of the grave marker and bowed her head down. She cried softly and Paul heard her say, "Please forgive me Robert, I don't hate you. I hate myself for not being able to be strong like you always were. Always were before........." Sara's voice trailed off without finishing the last of what she was saying, and she left her head resting on her arms as the tears flowed.

Paul walked over to her and placed his hand on her shoulder. She wasn't even startled when she felt his hand. She had actually been expecting one or both of her parents to eventually come and find her. Paul just said softly, "Honey, we need to go."

Sara stood up and started walking towards the car. Paul caught up with her and placed his arm around her shoulder, but she twisted away from him and ran to the car. She opened the back door and let herself in. A sudden feeling of panic started to creep over her as she sat and closed the car door. The feeling took her back to the previous night and sitting in the back of the police cruiser. Paul didn't make an issue of how she was acting. He was just glad to have found her safe, and that they could still get to the court in time. He called Susan on his cell phone and told her he had found Sara, and everything was fine; she was alright, and they were on their way home.

When Paul pulled into the driveway, Sara opened her door and jumped out before the car had even come to a complete stop. She walked quickly towards the front door and Paul called to her as he got out of the car. He was surprised at the look on her face as she turned around and glared at him. It was a look of anger and disdain he had never seen on his daughter's face, and one that he didn't understand. He thought to himself, *how could our perfect world have fallen apart so fast and so tragically.* He just watched as Sara hurried into the house.

As upbeat as he usually was, now he felt like he was losing hope. By the time he went inside the house, Sara had already gone up to her room and slammed the door.

Paul went up and knocked on her door. She didn't answer. He firmly said, "We have to leave in 5 minutes to go to the court. You don't have a choice Sara, so do whatever you need to do and get in the car, NOW!" He could hear her slamming some things around her room, and hoped she was getting ready despite what he heard.

Susan came through the front door as Paul reached the bottom of the stairs. "Where is she?" Paul told Susan that she was up in her room and that he had told her to be in the car within 5 minutes to leave for the court. Paul said, "I'm not sure what we are going to do. I pray the judge gives her a break since she has never been in any trouble before. I have no idea what community service they will have a girl that's only seventeen doing. To be honest though, the judge could even send her to one of the juvenile camps for who knows how long. Susan's mouth dropped open, and tears welled up in her eyes.

Susan grabbed both of her husband's arms. She shook him, crying out, "You can't let them take her away, you can't."

Chapter 14:

The Greene County Court was about 20 minutes away in Xenia, Ohio, the county seat. Sam Retherford, their friend and attorney was waiting outside the front door of the courthouse for them. As they came up the walk, Sam greeted them, "I was getting a little worried. I wasn't sure if you guys were going to make it on time." Sam looked at Sara and smiled. "Hi Sara, how are you doing?" As he put his hand out to greet her, Sara looked up at him angrily and simply hurried past. Sam looked at Susan and Paul and gave a sympathetic shake of his head.

They made their way through the security check and entered the lobby. Susan put her hand on Sam's arm as she asked, "So what happens now?" "Let's have a seat over here. Sara, I need to speak with your parents for a minute. Would you mind sitting over there on that bench down the hall? It will just be a minute." Sam pointed down the hall to an empty bench, and Sara walked over and sat down without saying anything.

Sam turned to Paul and Susan, and then looked back at Sara before saying, "Can I suggest we try a little shock effect for Sara?"

Paul and Susan looked at each other and then back at Sam. With a confused look on her face, Susan said, "What exactly do you mean?" Susan asked.

Sam continued, "Juvenile proceedings are private or one at a time. So, there won't be other cases or offenders, or anyone from the public in the courtroom when Sara goes before the judge. It's just a suggestion, but I have been told Sara's case won't be heard for another hour at least. It's not uncommon to have a delay like this. While we are waiting, why don't we take Sara into the adult court down the hall and let her think we are simply waiting for her case to be called in there. She will see the proceedings, and that'll give her the impression that is what she will be going through as well. She'll see prisoners brought in from the county jail that are awaiting arraignment. We might see cases ranging from drunk driving to assault, even manslaughter. Sometimes it's a sobering thing for someone who has never been in a courtroom and around sometimes hardened criminals.

That is not to say that these defendants are all bad people. Some are just here for failure to appear for a traffic violation.

There will be a variety of cases that will be brought before the judge. After a while, I'll just motion for all of us to leave the room, and then I'll lead all of you down the hall to the juvenile courtroom where her case will be called."

Paul looked over at Susan and she gave a nod of approval. Paul whispered, "Anything that might help shake her out of whatever she is going through." Sam nodded in agreement, "Ok, we'll go into the court room in a few minutes. They typically will bring in defendants that have been held in custody overnight. They will go through each of their cases one at a time. For the most part, it will be each one entering a plea of guilty or not guilty, and in some cases, no contest. Most likely after they go through those first cases, the judge will call for a short break. That's when we will get up and go wait outside the juvenile court room. A deputy at some point will come out into the hall and direct us inside to see the judge.

I will escort Sara to the front to face the judge. He will state the nature of the charges, and then he will ask how she pleads. What happens next depends on several things.

"With your permission, I would like to have a couple minutes alone now with Sara." Paul and Susan looked and gave a short nod at each other. "Okay, we'll wait here." Paul told Sam.

Sam walked over to the other bench where Sara was sitting. He sat down. "How are you doing Sara?" Sara rolled her eyes, shaking her head from side to side. "Okay Sara, you need to listen to me and listen very closely. Like I said last night at the police station, you better take this seriously. I know you're hurting, and I know you're angry." Sara jerked her head in his direction, "You don't know anything about me."

Sara turned her head back, staring at the wall across to the other side of the hall. Sam continued," It's true, I don't know everything you are going through or thinking, and I don't know what problems there are at home. None of that matters right now." Sam said firmly. Sam knew he needed to jolt her into reality. "Sara! Please. Look at me right now!" She slowly raised her head and looked at him. "You cannot go into that court room and show any kind of anger or attitude at the judge. If we are lucky, since you are a minor, you might just get off with community service.

"If you are respectful to the judge and don't have an attitude, it could be that and then restitution for the damages. Fortunately, the other girls that were with you admitted they were the ones that assaulted the officer. The prosecutor could still charge you as an accessory to that assault though. If that happens, you could likely be looking at some time in a juvenile correction facility. Trust me, that is not what you want.

Sara, no matter what else is happening in your life right now. With being taken out of school and that on your record, you could have a tough time getting your future back on track." Sara looked away as she made a grunting sound that was almost a laugh. She turned back and glared at Sam. There was a short pause and then she said each word slowly, in a low, angry tone, "I don't have a future." Then she turned away from him again. Sam put his hand on her shoulder and told her to look at him again. She did as she was told. "Sara, you do have a future, but let's not argue about that today. That's something you can worry about later, but we need to get the present handled right now. Let's go, we should be in the courtroom soon."

A few moments later, Sam stood and motioned for Paul, Susan, and Sara to follow him. He opened the door to the courtroom and led Sara in, with Paul and Susan following behind them. After a few steps down the center, Sara stopped and looked around the room. Paul hoped that the seriousness of what was about to take place was maybe finally settling in, and that she might realize she was in a courtroom, facing criminal charges. Charges that could drastically change her life, and not in a good way.

He wished he could get inside her head at that moment and just fix everything. He wished he could take away her anger, but most of all he wanted to soothe her pain. He wished he could get inside her heart and heal those wounds he knew were there. He knew this, because he had them too. He knew if he could help to eliminate her pain, that might take care of the anger. However, other than praying for his daughter at that moment, he wasn't sure of anything else he could do. He prayed silently, "Lord, this is in your hands. Help me to trust you."

Sara sat, showing no emotion on her face, staring at the back of the seat in front of her.

Her thoughts wandered to Robert. She dropped her head, looking down at her lap and imagining, *what would Robert think of me right now?* The anger quickly returned though, as she heard the door open towards the side of the room. Looking up she saw a deputy escorting several individuals in from a back room. She saw they were all dressed in the orange prison jumpsuits with numbers on the back, just like she had always seen on TV.

There were about fifteen of them total. She really was in a new, and unfamiliar world right now, and despite her efforts to stay stoic and sullen, she didn't like the feeling that was creeping over her at that moment.

Chapter 15:

After the last of the defendants had entered and settled in their seats, a door opened down front. The bailiff turned, facing everyone and in a booming voice exclaimed, "All rise, the Honorable Judge Daniel Guess presiding." Judge Guess stepped up onto his platform and told everyone to be seated. The judge went through rehearsed instructions to everyone in the room as to the seriousness of the proceedings and reminded everyone to remain quiet as cases were being heard. With that finished, the judge called for the first case to be read.

Sara didn't see who was speaking or where the voice was coming from because she was still staring over at the defendants who had been brought in from the back. "The first case Your Honor, is The State of Ohio versus Darrel Preston." A man in a three-piece suit stood up from the seating area and motioned towards the area where those in the orange jumpsuits had been brought in. She assumed the man was the attorney representing whoever was being called to the front, and she was correct. A sheriff's deputy escorted a young man to the front table facing the judge, and the man in the suit stood next to him.

Sara couldn't take her eyes off the young man. He looked about the same age as her brother Robert had been but looked as though he had lived twice the number of years Robert had. She couldn't help but notice the metal shackles around his ankles with just a couple feet of chain between them, allowing him to take moderate steps. His hands also were cuffed together. He had a tattoo of a dagger down one side of his neck, and several more along the same subject matter down both arms. One of his hands was covered with a tattoo depicting the skeletal bones of his hand. She felt a shiver run down her spine and swallowed hard.

Some of the new friends she had started hanging out with had a few tattoos, and she had thought about getting one just to make her parents mad. She thought about that very thing at that moment and wondered if her parents would even care. Would they even care about her, or just be mad about a tattoo on their precious little Sara, and then what their friends would think? Her choice of a tattoo, though, was a little fairy like Tinker Bell on her upper arm, or Thumper, the playful bunny rabbit with the big smile on his face. Then her eyes caught something. She stared at the young man right now standing before the judge.

Her eyes went wide when she noticed one arm, the young man had a Thumper tattoo. This Thumper though had a snarled look, holding a knife in one hand with blood dripping down from it. Suddenly, Thumper didn't seem like a great idea anymore.

All of these thoughts were shaken off when the judge began to speak. "Mr. Preston, you are charged with attempted murder, assault with a deadly weapon, resisting arrest, assaulting a police officer, driving under the influence of a controlled substance, and, finally, fleeing the scene of an accident. Do you understand the charges as read?" The man snorted, and in a quickened tone said, "yeah". The judge visibly rolled his eyes in an expression that said, ".... it's going to be one of those days." "How do you plead?" The judge asked. The attorney started to say something, but the young man shouted, "It don't matter. You're going to say I'm guilty anyways. So, screw you." The attorney was grabbing the young man's arm, telling him to stop. The judge began pounding his gavel on the bench loudly, demanding order.

The young man yelled, "Order? *Order this* old man." And with that, he thrust his middle finger at the judge.

The attorney closed his eyes, shaking his head back and forth in frustration. The judge pounded his gavel yet again and yelled, "Bailiff, get this guy out of my courtroom." The bailiff was already moving towards the young man and grabbed his arms from behind. Another deputy moved quickly to assist the bailiff, and they half-dragged the man towards the door they had brought all the men in the orange jumpsuits through at the beginning. The young man continued yelling profanities now at the judge. His last act of defiance was spitting towards the judge's bench. Most of the other men in orange, still sitting in their area on the side were smirking, and some were even laughing. The judge looked over at the group of men as he said, "I'm so happy you all find that so amusing. It's put me in such a good mood to hear each of your cases now. Bailiff, let's have the next case."

Sara sat wide-eyed, with her mouth half hanging open. Even in the pit of depression and anger she had allowed herself to fall into, she still knew in the back of her mind, one has got to show some respect to a judge.

Susan and Paul were just as shocked over what had played out in front of them.

Susan had her hand over her mouth, shaking her head back and forth. Paul looked over at Sam, and Sam gave a sideways nod towards the door, letting Paul know they could all go back out in the hall now.

Sam couldn't have scripted a better scene to give Sara a jolt into reality. There was no need to sit through the rest of the proceedings being heard before Judge Daniel Guess.

Sam put his hand on Sara's shoulder saying, "Come on Sara, we need to go out in the hall." The four of them stood and quietly moved towards the door at the back of the courtroom opened the door and went out. "Please wait here, I'll be right back." Sam said. Sam walked down the hall a short distance and stopped to talk to a uniformed officer. It really was just a show to make it look like he was asking the officer a question.

He returned, saying to Paul, Susan, and Sara, "Sara's case has been moved to Courtroom Number 3 down this way." Pointing in the direction of the other courtroom, he looked down at Sara before saying, "Come on, we need to sit outside that room and wait to be called." Sara was still in shock at what had happened in the other courtroom.

She didn't question what they were doing now. Sam suspected that Sara would think because of what had happened with the unruly defendant that they had moved some other cases to a different court room. He figured she might realize at some point that no juvenile cases would have been heard mixed in with adult cases, or before that judge. However, mission accomplished for now, thought Sam.

Susan stood up and walked down the hall to use the restroom. She had struggled to keep her composure after seeing what had taken place in the courtroom. She wanted to get away from Sara before she completely lost it. She went into the bathroom and immediately started breathing rapidly in and out, tears running down her cheeks. She closed her eyes and tried to get her breathing under control before she hyperventilated and passed out right there in the restroom. When she opened her eyes, she found herself looking down into the sink. She slowly raised her head and looked at herself in the mirror. A confused and defeated woman stared back at her. She felt a churning in her stomach and a knot in her throat. She quickly turned and just made it into one of the stalls before she threw up.

She returned to the sink, rinsed her mouth, splashed water on her face, then wiped the tears from her eyes. She made herself look as presentable as possible, but when she left the restroom, she was pale, and her eyes were red. There was no hiding the fact that she had been crying and wasn't feeling well.

Chapter 16:

A few minutes later, a uniformed officer came out of the courtroom door and looked over at Sara before saying, "Sara Tessler?" Sara looked up and just kind of raised her hand to acknowledge that was her. Sam the attorney stood and gently put his hand on Sara's arm to let her know it was time, her time to go into the courtroom now. Susan swallowed hard and took in a deep breath, hoping she wouldn't repeat her experience throwing up in the bathroom, this time in front of everyone. She was still a little pale and feeling weak in her knees as she stood up. Paul turned towards her, "Susan, are you ok?" She nodded her head slightly and said, "I'm good, let's go."

They walked into the courtroom and Sara was surprised to only see just one uniformed officer and a lady sitting at a table off to the side of the judge's bench. The judge was already sitting behind the bench. It was much different than what she had seen in the other courtroom, and she took in another deep breath, feeling somewhat relieved. Sam motioned for Paul and Susan to take a seat on the front bench.

He placed his hand on Sara's back, stopping her as she started to follow her parents. "You and I have to go to that table in front of the judge's bench." Sam said. They walked to the table and stood facing the judge. There were no chairs except at a table off to the side. Susan thought that was odd, but then thought that maybe that meant that this would be a quick procedure and they would be going home soon. She had never been involved or had even seen on TV a juvenile court proceeding that she could remember, she wasn't sure what was going to happen even if it was a short process.

Susan sat there thinking to herself, *will we be going home without Sara today? Is the judge going to have that officer handcuff her? Will we have to sit and watch them drag our daughter away with me screaming, don't take my baby!* She noticed she was breathing hard and more rapidly again, so she closed her eyes and tried to concentrate on her breathing, waiting for the judge to start speaking.

It was obvious that this was a much more casual setting and atmosphere. Susan thought perhaps that was on purpose since in this case it was dealing with a juvenile.

She didn't really know though since she thought again about the fact that she didn't have any experience with how the juvenile court did things.

The judge picked up a cup of coffee and took a sip. He set it down and looked at Sara, saying nothing. Sara remembered what Sam had told her about keeping her attitude in check. She couldn't bring herself at that moment to look the judge in the eye. She was focused on a spot on the front of the judge's bench, her gaze just below actually looking up at the judge directly.

The judge's name was Dean Montgomery, and he was considered one of the best at dealing with juvenile cases. He had a real compassion for teens and genuinely wanted to try and help steer them in a better direction in their lives. A better direction before they reached a point of no return and ended up standing before a judge in an adult court. He always wanted to do everything he could to prevent them from becoming just another statistic. He handled things differently than most other judges, those that handled juvenile cases. Most juvenile court justices had become jaded by the system. It caused many of them often to just go through the motions.

By contrast, Judge Montgomery regarded each teen individually. He did his best to help them if he could. That's why he took a more conversational tone at first.

The judge shuffled some papers in front of him, looking down and reading silently. He then raised his head and looked directly at Sara. In a soft tone, the judge said, "You are Miss Tessler, Sara, is that correct?" Sara knew now that she had to look him in the eye. She raised her head slightly and looked at the judge. She simply nodded her head. Sam gave a slight nudge on her back with his hand. Sara understood the meaning of what he was trying to convey and quickly responded, "Yes Sir."

What the judge said next surprised her and even caught her a little off-guard. He smiled and said, "Is it alright if I call you Sara?" She registered a slight look of surprise on her face, and responded, "Uh, Ok." She second-guessed herself right away and wondered if there was a better, or more respectful way she could have answered his question. His next question put her fears at ease, but once again threw her off a little.

"Tell me about yourself Sara." She felt a little bewildered, not sure how to answer.

She looked to Sam hoping he was going to tell her what to say. When Sam didn't offer any help, she looked back at the judge and nervously began, "Uh, I'm seventeen years old, and uh, I go to Bellbrook High School, and…" The judge held up his hand in a gentle motion, indicating he wanted her to pause.

The judge smiled and said, "No Sara, tell me about you. Tell me who Sara is right now at this point in her life. Be totally honest. Can you do that for me?" At this point Sara was again caught off guard and didn't know how to respond. She looked from side to side as if someone or something was going to give her the right words to say.

She thought to herself, *"What should I say? He said be honest, but I'm not sure I can do that. Do I tell him I'm angry? Angry at my parents who maybe didn't do enough to save Robert? Do I tell him that I'm so angry I have wanted to even take my own life so this pain can finally stop?"* Before she spoke, she saw the judge stand up and step down from the bench. Her eyes got a little wider as he approached her and Sam.

The judge smiled and held out his hand for her to shake. He said, "Sara, I am Judge Montgomery."

She slowly held out her hand and he grasped it firmly but not hard, and he shook it, saying, "I want to help you Sara, so let's sit." With that, he motioned towards the table and chairs that were just off to the side of where they were standing. She looked over at the table, then back to Sam. Sam motioned with his hand towards the table and chairs without saying anything.

The only thing going through Sara's mind at that point was she was thankful, thankful to sit down because she felt her knees shaking. She even thought she might fall as she started walking, but thankfully did not before she reached the table.

Chapter: 17

Paul and Susan sat staring to the front of the court room with their mouths slightly agape. They both thought to themselves that this is not what they were expecting. Paul wondered if the judge was just making Sara feel comfortable, setting her up so that later he could pounce at her with a booming voice and accusations of her being a juvenile delinquent, telling her that it was just a matter of time before she ended up in state prison. Instead, they felt more reassured than at any time since their friend, Police Chief Tomlinson had come to the door a couple of nights before. Susan glanced over at Paul with a slightly confused look on her face but didn't say anything.

Judge Montgomery pointed towards a seat on one side of the table, and Sara slowly lowered herself into the chair. The judge turned to Sam the attorney, "Mr. Retherford, do you mind if we sit and talk for a bit?" Sam gave a nod, "Not at all your honor."

The judge began to speak. "Sara, I got into some trouble when I was 16 years old, so I was about your same age. I don't need to go into the details, they're not important.

"However, afterwards, I got to a point where I thought my life was over because of what had happened. Life throws all of us some pretty crummy things sometimes, and it's hard not to react or act on those things. I realized at the time, even though my intention was to hurt myself, I was hurting those around me even more."

Sara just stared across the table without saying anything. She wanted to look back at her parents but didn't dare take her eye off the judge. The judge said, "So Sara, tell me what's going on in your life right now, please."

Sara swallowed hard and said, "I don't really know to be honest. My life was about as perfect as I thought it could be not that long ago." She looked down as she mumbled, "I don't care anymore." Judge Montgomery said, "I'm sorry, what was that last thing you said?" Sara let her emotions take over and she snapped back, "I said I don't care anymore." She immediately regretted raising her voice, and her eyes widened as she looked across at the judge waiting for him to lash out at her. Sara quickly said, "I'm sorry. It's just that I don't really care about much of anything anymore." Judge Montgomery shook his head slightly, "Don't be sorry."

He smiled and continued, "I asked you to be honest, didn't I?" She nodded her head up and down but didn't say anything more. "Sara, I understand you might have gotten into a little trouble the other night."

The judge paused, letting the question linger. He continued, "Is that an accurate statement?" Sara looked down, then swallowed hard. "I...I guess." She dreaded the next question she knew was coming and the judge did not disappoint her. "So, tell me what happened and why it happened." Sara's throat was tight. She looked over at Sam, and he just nodded and said, "Go on Sara, the judge is waiting." Sara looked back at the judge and began, "Well, I was walking downtown with some friends, and we were just hanging out. One of the girls said she had an idea and told us to follow her." Sara looked down at the table before continuing. "And then one of the other girls went up to the back door of the museum and broke the window in the door, and then reached inside and unlocked it."

The judge patted his hand light on the table before saying, "Did you think that was wrong for her to do that?" "I wasn't really thinking one way or another at the time, to be honest."

Sara was surprised at her blunt and candid answer. "Well, that's all I am asking right now is for you to be honest, so please continue." Sara took another difficult gulp before going on. "I...uh... we, we went inside. At first, we just walked around the different rooms. It was dark, so I think all of us turned on the flashlight of our phones.

Then one of the girls said something about her mother or something like that, and she smashed something. I wasn't sure what it was. That's when things got kind of crazy, and I guess...." Her voice trailed off, "We wanted to hurt things or someone I guess." The judge sat back in his chair a little, rubbed a couple of fingers across his chin and then sat forward again. "You wanted to hurt things or hurt someone?" Sara looked up at the judge and didn't say anything for a long while. Sara bit at her lower lip. "I wanted to hurt everyone." As her voice trailed off, the judge heard the last few words when she said, "Including me." The judge pressed his lips together and just nodded without saying anything for a moment. At the back of the courtroom, Susan put her hand to her mouth as tears welled up in her eyes. Paul put his arm around Susan and pulled her close to him. She leaned her head on his shoulder and cried silently.

The judge turned slightly in his chair and looked away a little as if pondering a response. "Okay, I understand, but now can you answer my other question?" Sara looked at him with a confused look on her face. "The other question?" Judge Montgomery said, "The why."

Sara scrunched her nose up and tilted her head, "That is the why, I wanted to hurt anything and anyone I could. I was mad, I was mad at my parents, I was mad at my brother, I was mad at the friends that I used to have that were always telling me it's going to be okay. But it's not okay, it's never going to be just okay. Nothing is ever going to be the same. I thought at the time that everything in this museum reminded people of the past, but I didn't want to remember the past. I didn't want to remember the things that were making me hurt. I…" She stopped there and just looked down at the table, and she began to cry softly. Sam put his hand lightly on her shoulder but didn't say anything. The judge stood up and walked over towards his bench, reached over the top and picked up a box of tissues. He sat back down and pushed the box over to Sara. She took one and wiped her eyes.

Judge Montgomery sat for a while without saying anything. He leaned forward, resting his chin in one of his hands. He waited patiently, just looking across the table at Sara. She finally looked up at him, wiped her eyes again and said, "That's about it." The judge said, "Ok, I appreciate you being honest, I know that was probably hard for you. I know there are more details about exactly what took place as far as damages to things and such.

I have a couple more questions for you and I again need completely honest answers to them." Sara sat waiting, looking across the table at the judge and had no idea what his next question would be.

It seemed like a full minute even though it was just a few seconds. Then the judge looked her directly in the eye, and in a very serious, but still soft tone asked his question. "Did you hit the officer that was injured, or encourage someone else to hurt the officer?" Sara opened her eyes wide and shook her head back and forth. "No! I didn't even know that had happened, but it wasn't me, I swear it wasn't! I'm sorry!"

"You're sorry?" Sara nodded her head in the affirmative this time, "I mean I'm sorry he got hurt."

Judge Montgomery tilted his head giving her a questioning look, "Why are you sorry? Didn't you want to hurt the officer? Didn't you say you wanted to hurt everyone? Did you not mean that?" Sara wasn't expecting that question and didn't know how to answer. She had to admit that she'd said she wanted to hurt *everyone*.

Sara looked across at the judge, "I don't know any more what I want. I know I am sorry that officer got hurt. I guess he didn't deserve that. I mean, he didn't, he didn't deserve that.

The judge stood up and waited for her to look directly at him. "I want to thank you for being honest." Then the judge walked back and stepped up on the bench to sit back in his chair. He moved some papers around again that were in front of him. He began to speak, and Sam started to stand up, but the judge said, "Counselor, you and Ms. Tessler can remain sitting if you'd like." Sam nodded and said, "Thank you your honor." Judge Montgomery began speaking again.

"Sara, I'll be speaking with the other girls you were with when this incident took place. I do look at each case and each person separately though.

"I want you to know that. You are fortunately a juvenile in the eyes of the law, and that gives me a lot of leeway, if I choose. A few more months and your situation might be totally different. I do look at people individually as I said, but I also must look at things as a whole and of course take the law into account. Mr. Retherford has probably told you that you in fact could face multiple charges, considering everything that happened on the night in question. Even if someone else caused the damages and someone else assaulted that officer. The assault on that officer is an extremely serious charge, even for a juvenile." The judge paused to let his last remark sink in a bit. Then he continued.

"That type of charge almost certainly results in the loss of a certain amount of an individual's freedoms. In the case of a juvenile, that typically means a youth prison or youth camp run by the county or the state. Or in the case of someone over the age of 18, time in the county jail at a minimum, or in the state prison if they received a sentence of more than twelve months. I say this Sara, to point out how serious this whole situation is, which I am sure you have some understanding of, and your parents and Mr. Retherford may have already explained to you.

"Looking at your date of birth here on the paperwork, if this incident had occurred a few months from now instead of the past few days, you would be down the hall in the adult courtroom. You would have crossed that invisible line where the State considers you to be an adult. Just a few months and your life could be very different right now, and not in a good way.

"I would like to ask you all to wait out in the hallway, and the bailiff will call you back in a little while." With that, Judge Montgomery began to stand without saying anything more, got up and walked through the door to the side of the bench and was gone.

When they were all back out in the hallway and sitting down, Susan looked at Sam, "What's happening now, why didn't the judge say what he is going to do." Sam put his hand on Susan's shoulder before responding. "I have a feeling possibly he wants to hear from the other girls involved first. I like this judge because he handles things different than many, and he does genuinely look at each person involved in a case separately. We just need to wait."

Sara had walked away and sat down at the end of the bench by herself. Her stomach was in knots.

When the judge had mentioned adult court, she quickly had images in her head what had happened just a little while earlier. The young man yelling at the judge, officers basically tackling him and pulling him out of the courtroom. She was fighting her feeling of nervousness, along with anger still deeply seated inside her heart. She was tired now and wanted to just go to sleep. She almost smiled when she imagined Robert saying, *"Now that guy that yelled at the judge, he was a real Dork."*

Chapter 18:

Judge Montgomery was indeed planning on dealing with the other girls first. He would question Janie, Debbie, and Stephanie who were also minors before making any decisions. Sara's other friend, Georgia, was the one from the group that was over age 18. That meant that she would be seeing a different judge down the hall because she would be appearing in adult court. Her one saving grace in this whole situation was that she apparently was not the one that struck the officer, sending him to the hospital. The downside to her situation was the law would look upon her as an adult. An adult should know better and would be viewed as having influenced minors to commit a crime. Basically, she would be guilty of the old, "contributing to the delinquency of a minor" charge.

That was one of the real flaws in the system. The reality was that this girl was just a few months older than the other girls and probably no more mature than the rest of them. As Judge Montgomery had said to Sara, a few more months and she would have been looking at a very different situation. By law though, Georgia was considered an adult.

She had crossed that invisible line Judge Montgomery had told Sara. That was, as an adult, she should have known better. Since she should have known better, the consequences of her actions could, and typically would be much more severe.

Excusing himself, Sam got up and walked around the corner. He was meeting with the couple who had sat across from Paul and Susan at the police station the night all of this had happened. Paul and Susan had introduced Sam to them since they remarked that they didn't know what to do and didn't have an attorney. Sam would be representing their daughter as well.

The same officer who had directed them into the courtroom earlier came out of the same door as before, looked at Paul and Susan and asked, "Do you know where Mr. Retherford is? The judge is ready for his next client." Paul told the officer that he had gone around the corner. The officer walked around the corner and just a few seconds later came back followed by Sam, the other couple, and their daughter. The husband had his arm around his wife's waist and seemed like he was helping to hold her up as she walked with him.

Susan looked at the mom and her heart ached for her because she looked pale and frightened. She knew the feeling of course.

Susan shifted her focus to the couple's daughter and was surprised to see that the young girl didn't appear to be scared or frightened like her mom obviously was. The girl had a venomous, hateful look, like she was ready for a fight. Susan's first thought was, *"Please, whoever you are, young lady, don't mess things up for Sara and the rest of the girls by upsetting the judge."*

Even though Paul and Susan had been a little confused by how the judge had started out handling things in the courtroom, they were comforted he had not come across as a hardened and heartless person. It didn't seem that he was ready to throw the book at anyone who came before him, but if this girl went in with an attitude and said some things that gave the judge a different impression of Sara and the other girls, who knew what might happen. Hopefully Sam, the attorney was right, and the judge wouldn't let this other girl's attitude influence his decision about the fate of their own daughter. A woman from inside the courtroom opened the door.

Paul and Susan assumed she was some type of clerk for the court. She came out holding several file folders. She walked up to Paul, Susan, and Sara before saying, "It's probably going to be about an hour before Judge Montgomery calls you back in. There is a waiting area with some vending machines around that far corner and down the hall if you would like to wait there. It might be a little more comfortable."

Susan didn't want to endure a whole hour before finding out the fate of their daughter. She didn't want to sit around just waiting. The longer the wait, the more agonizing it was for her. She knew she had no choice. She was resigned to the fact that all they could do was exactly that, just wait. They all got up from where they were sitting and went down the hall and around the corner to the area the lady had pointed them toward.

What seemed like an hour was only about twenty minutes that had gone by, and then Sam came walking through the door of the waiting room. He came over and sat down at the table where Paul, Susan and Sara were sitting. Susan was anxious to hear what had happened with the Dan and Julie's daughter Janie.

Especially since she had gone into the court room looking so angry. Susan wanted to know if Janie had made the judge upset. She looked at Sam and cautiously asked, "So how did it go with that other girl?" Sam shook his back and forth a couple of times.Then he answered, "I can't really discuss another client or their case even though she was involved in the same incident that is before the judge. I hope you understand."

Paul waved his hand towards Sam, "Of course Sam, we understand. Please, don't worry about it." Susan was disappointed but she knew Sam was right. It was that whole client/attorney privilege thing, she supposed. Susan looked down at the floor and shook her head slightly, thinking to herself that she never imagined ever having to sit in a courtroom for any reason. She especially never imagined having to discuss attorney client privilege, or arraignments, sentencing, or any other courtroom lingo having to do with anyone in their own family. The mom part of her though let her mind go wild with thoughts that perhaps things had gone bad in the court room with the other girl. She thought, *now things might not go well for their daughter.*

Susan tried to shake those thoughts from her mind. She looked down at the table and prayed silently.

Chapter 19:

Sam excused himself and said he would be back shortly. He left the room and went back to where the other couple and their daughter Janie were waiting down the hall. The reality was, it had not gone well when Janie had talked to the judge. Judge Montgomery had taken the same approach with her that he had with Sara. He started out in that Grandfatherly-like demeanor he had when he first spoke with Sara. Janie was having none of it though, and got off on the wrong foot from the very beginning when Judge Montgomery began in a friendly tone, "Can I call you Janie?" With a scowl, her response was, "Whatever." The judge raised his head a little and bit at the side of his lip, contemplating what to say next, or what approach to take. Sam supposed the judge was trying to compose himself so he wouldn't lash out at the girl. That wouldn't accomplish anything good, and Judge Montgomery knew that.

Sam had really been impressed with what seemed like Judge Montgomery's genuine desire to help the young people who came before his court.

He cringed when Janie had snapped back at the judge with her answer. Sam put a hand on her shoulder, but Janie jerked away from him. It didn't get much better from there on out with Janie and the judge. The judge had taken the same approach, having Janie and Sam sit down at the table, then coming down from his bench and sitting across from them.

Sam was a professional and did his best for every client, but some of his thoughts at that time mirrored Susan's. He hoped that Janie's behavior would not affect the judge's decision when it came to Sara. Sam had been friends with Paul and Susan for a long time and had known Sara pretty much since she was born, but he had to work just as hard for this client as he would for any other, friends or not.

After Janie, Judge Montgomery had one more girl to see. The wait was more than the hour Paul and Susan had originally been told it might be, and they were getting anxious. Since coming out of the courtroom, Sara had not uttered a word.

Even when Susan had asked her if she wanted something to eat or drink, Sara had just shaken her head back and forth to say no.

Paul and Susan would occasionally glance over at Sara, trying to figure out what she was thinking.

They wondered what was going through her mind. Neither of them could really tell if Sara was scared, nervous, or just ambivalent about the whole thing. They could tell that Sara was a little surprised at the judge's approach, taking more of a conversational tone with her. What they couldn't tell was whether Sara was pleased over how things had gone. Since the night of the incident, Sara had for the most part remained the same way she had been for the last year or more, short tempered, disrespectful, and in a sullen mood.

As it turned out, Sam's decision to first take Sara into the adult courtroom had worked as he had hoped it would. Sara had begun the day determined to maintain a rebellious attitude, even with the judge. She had even pictured herself staring down the judge in defiance of anything he was going to say to her. What she witnessed in the adult courtroom had given her pause and had knocked her off her game. As silly and destructive as that game was, part of her was doing everything in her power to win that game. A battle of conflicting emotions took place within Sara's mind.

She was still extremely mad at those closest to her. Her thoughts kept going back to Robert.

She wondered if he would have been disappointed in her or if he would have been mad at her for having changed the way she had. She thought how Robert had always told her how proud he was of her for all of her accomplishments in sports, cheerleading, and her grades. In her mind she scoffed at that thought and silently scoffed at that thought, "Screw you Robert, you lost your right to tell me anything." She replayed in her mind everything since that fateful night at the basketball game and all the emotions she had gone through since. The part inside that was fighting to keep her in her depressed state kept winning those small battles.

Sam returned to the lounge area they were in and said, "The judge is ready for you, Sara, but we have a few minutes." He looked at Paul and Susan, "Do you mind if I have a minute alone with Sara?" They were both a little surprised but didn't question his request. Paul told Sam that was fine and that they would be waiting outside the courtroom. Then he put his arm around Susan's shoulder and led her out of the room.

As her parents left the room, Sara looked up at Sam expressionless, wondering why he wanted time with her now. Sara's silent conversation with Robert had only served to put her back in the depressed state she had spent so much of the past year in.

That depression and distain showed when Sam put his hand on her shoulder and she jerked away, leering at him and saying, "Leave me alone." That confused Sam a little because up to that moment, Sara had not said anything like that or used that tone with him or anyone else. Sam was dealing with mixed emotions of his own at that moment. The part of him that had known the Tessler's for twenty years-plus or more, and Sara and Robert for pretty much their entire lives, wanted to give Sara a comforting hug. He wanted to tell her things would be alright. Then he recalled her words to the judge, *"I'm tired of people telling me it's going to be alright."* The professional side of him knew he had a job to do and that how he handled things moving forward in the next thirty minutes or so might be a determining factor in Sara's future. He suddenly felt an overwhelming burden and responsibility he had never felt before when representing a client. He knew he was a good attorney.

He had always done his best to represent his clients, and genuinely felt sympathy for any situation they were going through. Today was different for some reason, however. He had represented minors before, even other friends' children. As he sat this time and looked at Sara, though, the feeling made him uncomfortable on a personal level. He couldn't figure out what made this case so different.

Sam waited probably a half a minute before he began to speak. "Sara, I know you have never been in a real courtroom. I'm not sure what you expected, but you might have been surprised by how Judge Montgomery handled things in his courtroom. So far, how he is handling things is a big plus for you and your situation. From a professional standpoint, I can't go into details of the other case of your friend Janie who saw the judge after you did, but let's just say, it didn't put the judge in a very good mood. I want to reiterate what I had said before: how you act and interact with the judge when we go back in, might have consequences that affect you the rest of your life. I just want you to think about that for a little bit before we go in there.

"I am one that will never tell someone, 'I know how you feel.' Not unless I am going through or have gone through the exact or at least a similar situation. I say that to let you know, I really don't know how you feel. I've never been through what you are going through. Especially anything like what you've gone through the last year or more. It would be disingenuous of me to try and tell that I know how you feel, because I don't.

"I can't tell you exactly how you are supposed to handle your feelings and emotions. As your attorney, all I can do is give you advice on how you need to handle yourself right now in this setting." Sara had been looking away the entire time Sam was speaking to her. "Sara, I need you to look at me." He waited. It took a long moment, but Sara, a defiant look still on her face, slowly turned and looked at Sam. Sam pressed his lips together before starting again. "Sara, please try your hardest to put aside as much of that anger as you can when we go back into that courtroom. Deal with it however you are going to deal with it moving forward, but for the few minutes we are standing or sitting before Judge Montgomery, please do all you can to try to suppress it. Be respectful. That's all I am saying. Answer his questions without any attitude.

"Let's let this play out until he gives his decision. Can you do that for me, and for you?" Sara's lips were pressed tight together, and she fought the urge to tell him what she wanted him to do with his advice. She kept her lips pressed tightly, then narrowed her eyes a bit as she slowly nodded her head up and down. Sam said, "Ok, let's go. The judge will be ready for us to come back in soon."

Sam and Sara walked back to the hallway where Susan and Paul were waiting. Sara sat herself down on the far end of the bench a few feet away from her parents, and Sam remained standing. Susan was frustrated, confused, and just plain tired. She was ready to lash out at Sara but was trying desperately to control herself. Susan drew in a long breath before saying, "Sara!" It was a little louder and menacing tone than what she had meant to use. Sara turned and scowled at her mother.

Sam saw what was about to happen. If Susan got into an argument with Sara right then, it would only make matters more strained when they went into the courtroom in the next few minutes. Sam called Susan's name in a slightly friendly tone.

Susan turned to look at Sam and she understood the unspoken warning of, *"don't"*. Sam put his hand on Susan's shoulder and smiled, "I think we are just about to go in, and I think Sara is all set. We went over what comes next already." He smiled at Susan, and she understood that the *"already"* meant it was best for her to not get into any arguments right now with her daughter. Susan patted his hand still resting on her shoulder, "Thank you Sam, for everything."

Chapter 20:

The door to the courtroom opened and the bailiff stuck his head out, saying, "We're ready for you folks to come back in." Paul and Susan both took a deep breath at the same time and stood up. Susan reached out a hand to Sara, but Sara just looked at it and turned her shoulder away as she stood up. Susan fought back the tears that had been building up for some time and were threatening to burst out. Sam stood to the side and held out his arm, directing Paul, Susan, and Sara to go ahead of him as he held the door for them. Susan didn't know why, but as she sat down, she was more nervous now than she had been in the first part of the hearing when everything was unclear.

The courtroom was eerily quiet and then the silence was broken when she had heard the bailiff's announcement, "All rise." Then she watched the judge enter from the back door and walk up onto his bench. She noticed that the judge's eyes were on all of them from the moment they walked through the door, which only increased her growing anxiety. She suspected correctly that the judge was really watching Sara. Perhaps he was trying to judge her mood.

Susan wasn't sure, so she took another deep breath and said another silent prayer before sitting down.

Up to this point, Susan had been very pleased with how this judge had handled things and she just prayed that Sara wouldn't do something or say something to provoke him to anger. She had watched enough courtroom shows to see how a judge could change very quickly if a defendant lashed out at him or her, causing the penalty imposed to be much harsher than he or she might have originally intended. Susan just wanted this day to be over.

There was no formal reading of the name or case details. After they were all seated, Judge Montgomery motioned with his hand, saying, "Sara Tessler, will you please approach the front." This was obviously the serious part of the hearing and less conversational whereas before, the judge had a friendly tone. The judge's demeanor was serious and business-like. Sam stood and held his arm out towards the front of the courtroom to let Sara go in front of him. Sara felt numb but at the same time was still fighting a feeling of disgust for all of these adults around her, including the judge.

As she walked up the center of the court room, Sara felt like she was walking the last mile towards her execution. She was a young lady, not yet an adult, and often the bravado teenagers try to give off sometimes only lasts so long before the child in them returns and they exhibit genuine fear over a situation. She was fighting both emotions of anger and fear at that moment, which only added to whatever it was that she was feeling.

Judge Montgomery let Sara stand there for a moment before speaking. He shuffled a couple of papers around that were in front of him as he had earlier. He liked to make the defendant wait momentarily. In this type of setting, even only five or ten seconds of silence seemed like forever for the one waiting to hear their fate. This was intentional on the judge's part. He always felt that this forced the defendant to pay close attention and stay focused on what the judge was about to say. It worked to perfection as Sara stood there. Just like before, not wanting to look the judge in the eye, she let her eyes wander a little and thought to herself, *"Why isn't he saying anything?"* She looked over at Sam and he gestured his hand towards her, silently telling her to simply wait.

Judge Montgomery began. "Sara Tessler, do you know why you stand before this court?" Sara just stared at the judge, not knowing what to say. Sam put his hand on her shoulder and said, "Go ahead Sara, answer the judge." Sara looked down towards the floor and then back up to Judge Montgomery. "I, um." She paused just for a second and then, still not knowing what else to say, blurted out, "Because I broke the law." As soon as she said it, she silently chastised herself, *"That was a dumb thing to say, of course I broke the law. If I hadn't broken the law, I wouldn't be standing here."* Her tone had also sounded frustrated and that wasn't really her intention, despite how she really felt. The judge regarded her for a moment. Paul and Susan took in slow, deep breaths and prayed silently. It was too late to say anything more or clarify her thoughts as the judge said, "Well you broke the law, yes. Do you know what else you did, Ms. Tessler?" Sara's first thought was, *"He's not being as friendly because he's calling me Ms. Tessler instead of my first name."* Everything hit at that point, and her heart began to sink. She stood there frozen, and for the third time in less than a minute she was unsure how to reply. Judge Montgomery let the silence do its work.

After a moment, he continued in a serious tone, "I believe I asked you a question Ms. Tessler." Silence, dead silence. This time the judge just waited. A full fifteen seconds went by, which seemed like an absolute lifetime to everyone in the courtroom. Sara finally said, her voice shaking slightly "Um, I, I don't know what you mean."

Judge Montgomery pointed to the side where they had sat and talked earlier, "Ms. Tessler would you please go over to the table there and have a seat? The one where we first sat and talked." Sara looked at Sam and he extended his hand towards the table. Sam and Sara both went to the table and sat down. Sara watched the judge get out of his chair, step down and walk through the door to the left of the judge's bench, and disappear as the door closed behind him. Sam suppressed a smile. He figured he knew what the judge was doing, and he liked it. Sam once again felt the judge really did have a heart for kids and was making a special effort to break down the walls that surrounded Sara by making her wait and think.

Chapter 21:

It was about three or four minutes before the door opened and the judge came out again. Instead of stepping up onto the bench though, he walked over to the table and stood on the opposite to look down at Sara. From that position he towered over her, and to her he seemed ten feet tall. The judge then said, "Sara, before I ask you to stand before the bench again, you *will* have an answer to my last question, and that question was, what else did you do?"

With that, he turned and walked behind the bench where he stepped up on the platform and sat. He looked over at Sara who sat with a blank look on her face, and reminded her, "And your previous response, 'I don't know what you mean' is not an answer." Sam looked down at Sara and saw her swallow hard. The judge let a full minute go past as he again shuffled a few papers, picked one up as if reading it, and then took a drink from his water glass. The judge surprised Sara and really everyone else as he stood up, picked up a clean water glass, and with the small pitcher he had used before, walked over to the table where Sara and Sam were sitting.

He set the glass down and poured some water into it. He slid it over to Sara without saying anything and then returned to his bench. Sara cautiously took a drink. She set the glass down and looked straight at the judge, waiting for whatever came next. She knew she had to have an answer ready when he asked again. The judge let another full minute go by, then finally in a slightly elevated tone, "Ms. Tessler, will you please come here to the front."

Sara took in a slow deep breath and stood up. As she started to stand, she felt her knees buckle, but she regained her balance and stood. She walked slowly towards the judge's bench and stood before him. This time, instead of standing right beside her, Sam stood slightly behind her and to the side. He knew the judge wanted whatever she said to come from her, without relying on anyone else to direct her thoughts or words. The judge cleared his throat and then spoke, "Ms. Tessler, we've already determined that you most definitely broke the law, is that correct?" Sara gave a determined, "Yes!"

The judge continued, "In doing so, Ms. Tessler, do you know what else you did?"

Sara took in a slow, deep breath, closed her eyes for a second, and then a thought came to her. She looked at the judge and almost excitedly exclaimed, "I hurt other people."

She had been so relieved that she had come up with an answer, her words and tone sounded happy instead of how serious the situation and events had been. The judge slowly raised both of his hands, locked his fingers together and rested his chin on his hands. He looked down, pausing before responding to what she had said. He raised his head and cocked it a little to the side, "You did indeed, Ms. Tessler. I'm curious, do you know how many people you hurt?" Sara shook her head back and forth. The judge said, "I take that as a no." Sara affirmed, "No Your Honor, I mean yes, I mean." The judge raised his hand for her to stop, and he suppressed a smile, knowing he had succeeded in making her a little nervous.

"I'm not surprised that you don't. Far too many times, we don't understand the extent to which our actions reach beyond ourselves. Far too many times, they affect people we don't even know or have never even met.

"Sometimes it's hard to even imagine how many people our actions may impact, sometimes in a positive way and sometimes negatively. Would you say that is a true statement, Ms. Tessler?" Sara shook her head up and down and answered, "I guess." But quickly followed her words with, "I mean yes." The judge said, "You are a student, is that correct?" Sara nodded again as she answered, "Yes", and he acknowledged her answer with a closed lip, "hmm."

The judge rested his chin on his thumbs with his forefinger across his lips and staring intently at Sara. He cleared his throat again, "I understand one of the subjects you are majoring in is history, is that correct?" Once again, Sara responded with a simple answer of, "Yes."

Judge Montgomery continued, in a tone sounding much more serious than it had in the earlier exchanges, and more directly as he stated, "Yet you, for reasons we have yet to understand, participated in vandalism, trying to destroy pieces of history. Artifacts of the history of your own community of Bellbrook." The judge said more firmly, "You were born in the town from what I understand.

"You attempted to destroy part of Bellbrook's heritage. I'm struggling to understand why a person interested in history would do such a thing.

You broke into a building, and not just a building, but one of the historic structures that has survived nearly two hundred years or more in Bellbrook. You vandalized and defaced antiques and relics.

"As I understand it some of those items had been in the town of Bellbrook since its founding. Many were on loan from private homes and were pieces of those family's heritages, heirlooms that belonged to their ancestors.

"While you may not have done so personally, you were also part of an assault on a police officer." Sara could feel her throat constricting as she recalled the incident. The judge continued, "Ms. Tessler, do you know who Marty Gibson is?" Sara thought for a moment and wasn't sure if this was someone she was supposed to know or not. She finally remarked, "No sir not that I can think of."

The judge nodded and said, "I see." He paused for just a moment and then continued, "Mr. Retherford has probably explained something in particular to you Sara.

154

"So, you may have already an understanding - everyone participating in a crime is, and should be considered, an accomplice to anything and everything that happens. There are plenty of people that are even serving life sentences today for being an accessory to murder even though they were not the ones that pulled the trigger or drove the car that killed the victim. Ms. Tessler, do you know someone named Carol Gibson?" Sara once again, shaking her head back and forth admitted, "No sir."

The judge in a very serious but surprised tone asked, "You mean you have never met Carol Gibson?" Sara looked towards the floor, trying to think of who Carol Gibson was, or Marty Gibson for that matter. She wondered whether that was one of her friends' parents. She realized she didn't even know any of her newer friends' last names or who their parents were. She finally raised her head back towards the judge and said, "I'm sorry, I can't remember if I know who that is."

The judge said, "Well you most certainly know who Mr. and Mrs. Berryhill are, don't you?" The name Berryhill sounded familiar to Sara because she had seen it on a few grave markers in the Bellbrook cemetery. She nodded her head up and down.

She quickly responded then, saying to the judge, "I've heard that name before, but don't really know anyone. I mean, at least not that I can think of." Judge Montgomery continued, "Ms. Tessler, I have read in the police report from the incident in question about the items that were damaged in the museum. There was a lamp that was broken, as well as a wooden bench that had part of the back broken off. There was a very old doll that had its head torn completely off.

"There was profanity written on the bench with a red magic marker, as well as on the walls and other items. That lamp and bench, Ms. Tessler, belonged to Mr. and Mrs. Berryhill. They had loaned those items to the museum for display. Those two items were passed down to them from their third-generation great-grandparents who were some of the first settlers in the town of Bellbrook. The Berryhill's ancestors are buried in the town cemetery. Do you know that those pieces of history, those pieces of the Berryhill's family heritage most likely came to the town of Bellbrook in horse-drawn wagons almost two hundred years ago?" Sara wasn't sure if she was really supposed to answer that question, and she was relieved when the judge continued.

"Ms. Tessler, you said you didn't know who Carol Gibson was. Is that correct?" Sara nodded and then remembered to say, "Yes, I don't know who that is." The judge nodded his head saying, "Uh huh", and then paused before continuing with, "Ms. Tessler, Carol Gibson is a little girl. A little girl whos' father is a police officer, and the other night cried herself to sleep, worrying about her daddy who was at the hospital because he had been injured responding to a call. Yes, Ms. Tessler, her daddy was the officer one of your friends assaulted that night."

Susan and Paul both sat forward with their mouths slightly open at this revelation. They had not heard really the extent or full details of what had happened in the museum that night and the actual damage that was done. They both could not imagine their daughter participating in something like that, but they knew very well that she had. Whether she had been personally responsible for the actual damage or not, she was still there, and was just as guilty. Susan couldn't stop the tears this time, so Paul pulled her tighter and leaned his head against hers.

Judge Montgomery continued, "If the article that was thrown at the officer had hit him in just the right spot, he very well could have died. That, at the very least would be classified as manslaughter, Ms. Tessler, and could have caused you to spend a significant amount of the rest of your young adult life in prison"

With that statement, Susan's hand went to her mouth, and the tears blurred her vision to the point she could not even focus on the front of the courtroom anymore. Susan thought for sure the judge was about to tell her little girl that he was sending her to a juvenile facility or camp. Paul leaned down and whispered, "It's going to be okay." The only thing was, he wasn't sure that what he had just said was true or not. He had the same thought as his wife from the judge's last remark. He thought to himself, *"Was their little Sara, their sweet Sara going to end up in a youth prison?"* Susan and Paul both knew if that happened, it most likely would mess her life up even more, and possibly permanently destroy any chance of her getting back to the intelligent, fun, vivacious young lady she had been before she lost her brother. They both bowed their heads in silent prayer. They had lost count how many times they had pleaded with God just that morning.

Sara watched the judge shake his head back and forth, his lips drawn in tightly together. To her it wasn't a look of disappointment, it was more a look of disgust. She had a lump in her throat now and swallowed hard again. Judge Montgomery folded his hands together and this time, rested his forehead on them. He raised his head and looked at Sara without saying anything for a moment.

Then he spoke. "Ms. Tessler, one thing in your favor right now is this is your first offense of any kind. I am taking that into account with my decision as to what to do. Also, fortunately for you, the young lady who was responsible for the assault on the officer fully admitted to having done so. Had she not been willing to take responsibility for that action, I might have had no other choice but to hold everyone involved responsible, including you, Ms. Tessler. Someone assaulting a police officer most likely land in jail for a significant amount of time, or in your case, as I mentioned before, in a juvenile facility to be determined by this court. You are close enough to your eighteenth birthday Ms. Tessler, that after serving the first part of a sentence in the juvenile facility, you would most likely be transferred to the adult county jail.

"There you would serve out the remainder of your time. Ms. Tessler, you may consider yourself fortunate that I am not holding you responsible for that assault." Sara's mom realized she had been holding her breath and when the judge said the last statement, her shoulders relaxed, and she let out a long slow breath of air. Paul did the same.

Judge Montgomery continued. "Ms. Tessler, earlier you admitted that you broke the law and that your actions hurt other people, and one of those people was physically injured. Do you still admit to having done so, Ms. Tessler? Sara forced the lump from her throat away and swallowed hard before saying, "Yes sir." The judge paused for a moment again and then, nodding his head, continued.

"Ms. Tessler, it is the determination of this court that in total disregard for the law and for others, you are responsible for breaking and entering at the Bellbrook Historical Museum.

It is also determined that you are responsible for the damage to historical artifacts belonging to the museum. "You are also personally responsible for damage of items belonging to other residents in your community.

"Finally, you are responsible for vandalizing the inside of the premises, in total causing multiple thousands of dollars of damage."

The judge paused to let what he had just said sink in a bit. He looked down at the papers he had picked up. When he looked back up, he focused his eyes directly on Sara's and pronounced, "Ms. Tessler, I am sentencing you to six months in the Greene County Juvenile Camp." Both of Sara's parents' eyes went wide and this time, even Paul's eyes welled up with tears. Susan let out a gasp of air as she clasped her hand over her mouth. At the front of the courtroom, Sara tried to swallow but couldn't. Sam put his hand on Sara's shoulder, and this time she didn't try to jerk away.

The judge continued, "What you did, you did so with willful disregard for the pain your actions caused to other people. You not only are responsible for the monetary value of the items vandalized, but their historical value. Those items, once destroyed or defaced, even if they *can* be repaired will never be the same. "Their originality and uniqueness are lost forever. It is hard to put a value on that aspect, but a value we must.

The court is fining you $5000 towards the repair, refurbishing, or replacement of the items that were damaged, as well as any damage to the premises. This court is fining you an additional $5000 towards the medical expenses of the officer who was hurt during this incident. I am also ordering you to serve no less than 40 hours' community service. The community service will be determined within one week from today and will commence no later than one week after that. I will decide when and where that community service will take place. If the 40 hours of community service is not completed to this court's satisfaction, an additional 40 hours will be imposed.

"The hours will continue to be added until this court is satisfied. Ms. Tessler, do you understand everything I have just said?" Sara, her bravado gone, fighting back tears of her own, answered with no emotion, "Yes."

The judge shuffled a few papers around in front of him, and again rested his chin. He took a deep breath himself and said, "Ms. Tessler, will you and Mr. Retherford come forward to the front of my bench." Sara turned her head and looked at Sam. He held out his right hand, motioning towards the judge's bench.

They both took several steps until they were directly in front of the judge. Sara felt her hands starting to shake and fought to keep them still. She tried again to swallow but her mouth had gone dry.

The judge waited a moment after Sara had reached the bench and looked her directly in the eye. "Ms. Tessler, I am suspending that portion of your sentence requiring you to serve six months in the Greene County Juvenile Camp. You are hereby placed on probation for a period not to exceed the date of your 18th birthday. If you are brought before this court for any offense prior to that date, you will be remanded to the Green County Juvenile Detention Center where you will serve out your full sentence, with no exceptions. I trust Ms. Tessler, I will never see you in this court again." With that, the judge slammed his gavel down with a thundering clack on the sound block. He rose without another look towards Sara, stepped down, walked through the door to his chambers and closed the door.

Chapter 22:

A mix of emotions ran through Sara, and her knees felt weak. The personal demons that had controlled her emotions for more than a year were fighting hard to keep control and come back to the surface again. The outrage that had guided her steps since Robert's accident was literally blurring her vision at that moment. Another part of her wanted to run to her parents and hug them tight and cry in their arms. At the present moment though, she was numb and did not know exactly what to say, do, or feel. Sam broke the brief silence as he once again placed his hand on her shoulder while saying, "Sara, I think you are very lucky. The judge gave you a great opportunity, a second chance. Please take advantage of that."

He held out his hand to guide her towards the back of the courtroom where her parents were already walking towards her. When Susan hugged her daughter, Sara let her arms hang limp and did not hug her back. Susan's heart was breaking for her daughter, but she had nothing more to say at that moment except, "I love you, sweetheart." She backed away to let Paul stand in front of her.

He placed his hands up on top of Sara's shoulders and said, "We are here for you, and we will get through this together. We love you." Sara did not look up at her father, only gave a disgusted snort through her nose and walked past her parents and through the door. Apparently, some of her demon's had won a small battle at that moment.

Paul and Susan made their way out of the courthouse. They could see Sara standing next to the car, waiting. Paul and Susan turned to Sam, and Susan gave him a hug saying "Thank you for everything, Sam. I hope everything works out for that other young girl. Is it okay if I reach out to her mother?" Sam smiled saying, "Of course. It's just that I can't discuss her case, but I am sure she would appreciate you contacting her. If she chooses to discuss what happens in the court with their daughter, that is totally up to her." Paul shook Sam's hand and thanked him as well, also offering a hug.

On the drive home, nobody said anything. Sara had a feeling of déjà vu as she sat staring out the window from the back seat. She was thinking back to the night that started this ordeal of being arrested.

She thought of her ride in the back of the police cruiser. Susan sat looking down at her hands resting in her lap. She knew they still had a long road ahead to try and save their daughter. Hopefully they could bring her back to some semblance of what she had been. Susan closed her eyes and silently prayed for their little girl, their little girl who before everything happened was a beautiful, vibrant and talented young lady.

There was very little communication or interaction over the next several days. Susan and Paul wanted to give some time to let things settle. The last few days had been a nightmare and they didn't want to make things worse by jumping on Sara with a laundry list of demands. For Sara's part, she mostly stayed in her room. The one thing Paul and Susan had told her was that at least for the time being, she was to have no contact or communication with the other girls involved in the incident. Her parents had taken away her cell phone as well. They changed the password on the Wi-Fi so she couldn't use the internet to contact any of the other girls that way. They told her all of this was temporary, and thankfully, Sara had not said anything back to them.

The next several days were a struggle for Paul and Susan to stay calm. They had talked with each other about sitting down with Sara to try and finally discuss things. They both worried, though, that they would lose their patience and blow up at her. They knew that this would only make things worse and push Sara further away from them. Somehow, ... They knew they had to start the process. They made Sara have meals with them and tried to engage her in regular conversation around the table. It all seemed disingenuous though, no matter how hard they tried.

At dinner on the third night after the day in court, they told Sara they all needed to talk after they were finished eating. Susan noticed Sara roll her eyes and sigh. No matter, though - they knew it was time. They weren't even sure what some of the ground rules should be moving forward, and their fear was whatever they did or said would drive her even further away. They were determined though, to do whatever was necessary to help their daughter.

They all three sat in the living room after dinner. Sara sat by herself with her arms crossed, staring at the wall across the room.

Paul and Susan sat together on the sofa. Sara's dad spoke first, "Sara, I owe you an apology." The expression on her face didn't change, but she turned her head to look at her father.

Paul continued, "I am truly sorry I haven't been a better example during the past year or so. I haven't been strong for our family." Sara cut him off angrily, "You mean, what's left of it. Right Dad?" Paul remained calm as he continued, "No Sara, our family is still here. Robert's memory is still part of our family; we will never let that go. You can't let that go. So, I do owe you and your mom an apology for what I've done. My arguing with you and your mother and getting angry with you when I should have done whatever I could to lift you both up." He turned to look at Susan and said, "I'm sorry, sweetheart." He looked at each of them asking, "Will you both please forgive me?"

There was a moment of silence and Susan squeezed her husbands' hand, "Of course Paul." Then squeezed his hand a little tighter. She looked over at Sara and said, "Honey, I owe you an apology too. I let my anger get the best of me and took it out on you and your father. Will you forgive me?"

Sara looked at her mother, then over to her dad. She looked back at Susan and narrowed her eyes saying, "I suppose it's my turn to give a big apology now, is that right?" Susan leaned forward and Paul could tell she was about to lose her cool. He quickly put his hand on his wife's arm to stop her. He said, "No, Sara. I hope at some point you do feel sorry for the things you have done recently to hurt people, but we can't make you do that. The main thing we both wanted to say this evening is that we are sorry for what we've done, and hope that you can forgive us. You can go on to your room now if you want."

Sara looked confused. She thought for sure they were both going to yell at her. She stood up, looked again at them both, and then walked towards the stairs. Paul called to her, "Sara!" Sara turned around. Her dad smiled saying, "The new Wi-Fi password is "You're a Dork." That caught Sara off-guard, and she nearly cracked a smile, then turned to start up the stairs. When she was halfway up the stairs, she heard her dad again, "Hey! that's dork with a capital D." Sara paused at the top of the stairs and allowed herself a half smile, then continued to her room.

The next day, a call came from the court telling Paul and Susan that on that coming Wednesday at 10:00 AM, Sara needed to come to the court administration office for details on her community service that was to begin the following week. They both thought, "At least this will get Sara out of her room."

They also hoped this could begin the path back to some normalcy and much-needed healing for their daughter and their family. Paul and Susan had not pressed Sara for serious conversation. They decided at least for now to let things play out and nature take its course. They would continue to pray and hope something would take place to bring their Sara back to them.

When Wednesday morning came and they were ready to leave for the court, Sara appeared and acted the same as she had for the last week or more. Distant and indifferent would be the best way to describe her. As the three of them walked up to the courthouse, Susan put her hand on Sara's shoulder and said in a pleading tone, "Sara, please don't question whatever it is they tell you to do." Sara looked sideways at her mother with a look of disdain and said under her breath, "Whatever!"

They entered the administration office and introduced themselves to the lady at the front desk. The lady asked them to have a seat, and someone would be right with them. A gentleman walked through a door on the side of the office but did not acknowledge them at first. The three glanced at the man, and then Sara made a double-take. She did not recognize him at first because the man was wearing a sport coat and tie, but it was Judge Montgomery. When the judge recognized the three of them, he stopped. Judge Montgomery looked down at Sara and greeted her with, "Good morning., Sara, how are you doing?" Sara opened her mouth to say something, but it seemed nothing would come out. She finally said, "Uh, I'm okay." The judge gave a nod towards Paul and Susan and said, "If you'll excuse me, I'm going to be late for court. No rest for the weary, I suppose."

As he started through the door into the hallway, he paused. He turned back and looked directly at Sara, and with a smile on his face, saying "Sara, you'll do a good job with your community service won't you?" He didn't wait for her answer but nodded again, stepped into the hallway and closed the door behind him.

The secretary stood and said, "Ms. Grimes will see you now", pointing towards one of the office doors to the side. She opened the door for them, and they walked into a modest- sized office. Ms. Grimes stood from behind her desk and asked them to have a seat. She introduced herself, saying, "I am one of the court administrators that handles community service.

Yours, Sara is somewhat unique, as minors are not always assigned community service. However, Judge Montgomery obviously had his reasons and, well, here we are. Judges are not necessarily involved directly in what or how the community service is carried out, but in this case, Judge Montgomery made a specific request." That did not make Sara feel very comfortable, even though for the most part the judge had been somewhat friendly. Sara remembered his parting words a few minutes earlier, *"You'll do a good job with your community service, won't you?"* She realized it was more of a statement than a question he had made, or even a warning.

Ms. Grimes handed Paul a paper as she instructed them, "Judge Montgomery has requested Sara to be assigned to assist someone in the retirement community.

Sara, you have forty hours to complete, and those will be done from 10:00 AM to 4:00 PM for the next seven Saturdays." Sara looked down and gave a slight groan, and thought to herself, *"Great, forty hours being a slave to old people."*

Ms. Grimes smiled and looked at Paul and Susan adding, "Will there be any conflicts with that schedule?" Susan was the first to say, "No, not at all." Paul remarked, "We will work around whatever is needed." "Excellent!" Ms. Grimes commented. She wrote down something on a notepad, and then tore the sheet off and handed it to Sara, saying, "Sara, this is the address you will be going to this coming Saturday. Unless you hear otherwise from someone here at the court, you will continue with your community service at that address every Saturday until the hours are fulfilled. That would be seven consecutive Saturdays. Do you have any questions?" Sara just shook her head. She heard her father clear his throat and knew the meaning. "No Ms. Grimes, thank you." Sara said politely.

Saturday morning came, and Sara had resigned herself to the punishment she would have to endure.

She was not thrilled about having almost two months of her Saturdays taken up. She admitted that her punishment by the court could have been much worse. She hadn't had any contact with the other girls involved since their late-night escapade at the museum and had no idea what happened with their court cases.

The address was in a 55-and-over retirement community. Paul pulled into the driveway and stopped, then turned to Sara before saying, "I'll pick you up at 4:00." Before Sara closed the car door, Paul called out, "Hey!" When Sara turned to look back in the car he said, "I love you." Sara stared at him briefly, then turned away without saying anything.

Paul waited as Sara stepped up onto the porch and rang the doorbell. He had expected his daughter's community service to be at some city office or community center, or someplace like that. He was a little wary of dropping her off at someone's house. He wondered what kind of community service took place at somebody's home. He trusted the judge, though, and it seemed Judge Montgomery personally knew what Sara was going to be doing to fulfill her hours of service.

It was then he saw an older, very distinguished - looking lady answer the door, and it put his mind at ease.

Part Two: Meet Jill Vincent Pay Oliver

Chapter 1:

The lady smiled as she opened the door and held out her hand. "You must be Sara. My name is Jill." Sara rolled her eyes upward, not moving her head to look at Jill. She raised one side of her upper lip with a look of disdain, then dropped her gaze to Jill's outreached hand without making a move to shake it. "Come on in Sara." She stepped back and motioned Sara into her living room area. "Make yourself comfortable Sara. If you will excuse me for a few minutes, I need to get a few things from the closet in the other room." Jill walked out of the room and down a hallway while Sara waited, feeling awkward.

Sara looked around the room and decided it looked normal for an older person's home. Across the room, she saw pictures lay out on a table. She walked over and looked down at probably a couple dozen or more pictures.

Most of the pictures were older black and whites with a few colored photos mixed in. There were also several of what looked like homemade cards, and some type of needlepoint or stitching of some kind on a piece of what looked like burlap.

Jill walked back into the room with a box and set it down on the table where the pictures were laid out. She turned to Sara saying, "Sara why don't we sit over on the sofas for a bit. Can I get you a glass of water or iced tea, or something else?" Sara shook her head no but didn't say anything. Jill tilted her head, smiled, and stared at Sara." Sara rolled her eyes again and said a little sarcastically, "No, thank you." Jill simply smiled. "Well just let me know if you change your mind." Jill walked over and sat down in a chair, then motioned for Sara to sit down on the sofa. Instead of sitting on the end closest to Jill, she walked to the middle of the sofa and sat down there. Jill studied Sara for a moment before remarking, "I assume Sara you don't really want to be here, and I understand that.

"But my dear, why don't we make the best of it since we are going to be spending a bit of time together."

Sara gave a look of disgust and blurted out, "Exactly why am I here?"

Jill smiled again saying, "Well as I understand it, you got into some trouble and, well, you have to spend some hours doing community service. That's about it, right?" Sara gave a huffed sound in reply as she sarcastically remarked, "Fine, so you know all about me right?" "No, I don't know all about you. I know very little about you. However, I do want to know who it is that will be helping me, and that's why I wanted to sit and talk for a bit. Sara shook her head with a mocking air and said, "Okay fine! I'm seventeen years old, I'm a senior in high school, and the last two years, my life has been pretty crappy. Nothing will ever be the same and there's nothing you, or I can do about it. So, I'm not a real happy person at this point in my life." Her voice trailed off a bit before saying, "I doubt I'll ever be happy again." Her voice returned to a normal level as she finished with, "In fact, I'm pretty much miserable most of the time. So that's me. Okay?"

Jill's look was serious but in a compassionate tone responded with, "Well, life does have its disruptions, there is no doubt about that.

"So, I think I can say I know how you feel." Sara jerked her head towards Jill and glared at her, saying, "Don't you dare! Don't you dare sit there and give me that phony line everyone uses, *Oh I know how you feel.* You have no idea how I feel, lady." Sara looked around the room then, taking stock of several of the items and decorations sitting atop Jill's tables and shelves before saying, "I seriously doubt you have had everything taken away from you. Everything you knew or cared about ripped away from you. People and things, taken away, and there was nothing you could do about it." Sara felt herself starting to cry but choked it back before continuing. "Is that what you would call a 'disruption'? I doubt it, so please don't tell me you know how I feel."

Chapter 2:

Jill looked at Sara and half smiled, and then she dropped her head slightly without looking Sara directly in the eye. Jill waited a moment, looked up again saying, "Sara, one of the things I have always tried to follow in my life is this: No one should ever tell someone 'I know how you feel' unless they have been through at least some similar experiences." Jill paused and looked as though she was considering her next words very carefully. She began, "I did, in fact, have everything taken away from me. It's not something I like to remember or talk about. To be honest, that's one reason you are here. Sara's eyebrows raised slightly with a confused look on her face as Jill continued. "My life was turned upside-down and many of the things and people I knew were taken away from me. Some of those people, I never saw some of them again, and just like you, there was nothing I could do about it."

Sara looked around the room and said, "I don't know how old you are, but it looks like you've lived a pretty good life." She followed that remark in a patronizing tone, "So it wouldn't appear as though you have had much of a big disruption to me."

Jill looked around the room herself before saying, "Oh, I've really been blessed. I have had a wonderful life, really, for the most part after my earlier childhood. Yes, I have had some disappointments most certainly, as we all do through life. I've been wronged by others at times, as we all have most likely. I've realized though - I am, or I should say, we are who we are because of all our experiences. The good and the bad, and it really depends on how we react and continue with life after those experiences. I have wonderful family and friends. I have many great memories over the years of the things I've done and the places I've seen. I also have some horrible memories. A lot of those are the ones that I would love to forget. You never forget though, not really. You hide them away in the back of your mind."

Jill paused again for a moment, and Sara thought she saw her maybe wipe away a small tear that was about to fall. Jill smiled slightly, still pondering what she was going to say next. Jill reached for her glass and took a sip, then cleared her throat, and continued.

"When someone says, *"Time heals all wounds"*, I have often thought, yes - wounds can be healed, or at least mended.

"You know, though, there's almost always a scar to remind you occasionally of what happened. That doesn't mean my life didn't have some of those, ah, disruptions as I called them. I would not want to live through your exact disruptions, and I know you wouldn't want to live through mine, I can assure you of that."

Sara was still more or less glaring back at her, annoyed with Jill's comment of *"I know how you feel"*, hanging in the back of her mind. She took a deep breath and let it out in a huff. She looked at Jill with disdain before continuing. "Well, looking around, I doubt your, uh, 'disruption' was all that bad." Jill took a moment to look down at her folded hands in her lap, and then back up at Sara. She leaned slightly towards Sara and in a soft, tender tone conveyed, "I have lost loved ones over my lifetime, and very early in life I had almost everything taken away. Ripped away from me like you described yourself. Our home was taken away from us.

Our car was also taken. Then, my mother, father, younger brother and myself were sent to a camp in Germany in 1942."

Sara's glare turned into a puzzled look. She held her hands up in a mock gesture of surrender, and she said, "I'm sorry, I didn't know you were Jewish." Jill gave a light laugh and said, "Oh, I'm not Jewish." There were more than just Jewish people in those camps. When the Germans occupied where we lived in Great Britain, they eventually deported many on the island as well as my family and myself, to the camps."

Sara thought back to some of her studies and her love of history. She had read with interest a few books on WWII for a term paper she worked on for school. Sara stared at Jill for a moment. She narrowed her eyes, with a questioning look remarked, "I do know some history and I also know that the Germans never occupied Great Britain." Sara, unconvinced, continued, "So I'm not sure I really understand since Germany never took over England." One side of Jill's mouth turned up a little and she gave another small laugh under her breath again. Jill shook her head back and forth and corrected Sara by saying,

"A lot of people don't know anything about the Germans taking over part of Great Britain.

"You are correct that the Germans never occupied the mainland. I mean the mainland of England. There is, however, a very sad chapter of our British history. It is a part that a lot of Brits don't want to remember, and many younger Brits sadly know nothing of it. We lived on Guernsey, one of the Channel Islands." Sara interrupted her to offer, "I've heard of the Channel Islands. I couldn't name them right this minute, but I do know they are part of Great Britain."

Jill smiled and continued, "Exactly! They are part of Great Britain, but when the Germans moved into France and the war was getting closer, the British government abandoned the Islands. They withdrew all the military that had been protecting the Islands, leaving the citizens to fend for themselves. Many citizens left if they could and went to the mainland, to London or other places there. Most were left to wonder what in the world was going to happen, and part of our family were among those. My two older brothers did make it over to the mainland, though." Sara had a confused look on her face. She tilted her head as she stared back and Jill.

Sara then said surprisingly, "Wait a minute - that war was about eighty years ago." Jill held up her hand to interrupt her. "Yes, and for myself from when I was living on Guernsey, it is eighty-seven years ago this year. I was 6 years old when the Germans took over the islands of Guernsey, Jersey, Sark and Alderny." Sara sat back, having set aside her combative demeanor, and she listened with interest as Jill continued.

"Several people have asked me to write about my story Sara, but I have not really wanted to go there. Also, the fact that I am not a writer, that is part of the reason I have not done so. That is in part where you come in, Sara." Sara gave Jill a quizzical look. Jill continued, "I was told you love history, is that correct?" Sara shrugged her shoulders, looked away, saying in a soft tone "Yeah, well I used to love a lot of things." She turned back to face Jill saying, "But anyway, what's your meaning?" Jill started by saying "I know how you…" but stopped herself before she said the word "feel" and then continued, "I'm sorry, I just!" Sara held up her hands again in a mocking look of feigned surrender, "I get it!" Jill smiled, "Sara, our time together, you will be helping me sort through pictures and in general, help me tell my story."

Sara had a confused look on her face and tilted her head slightly to one side before saying, "Um, Okay." There were a lot of different thoughts going through Sara's mind. She only knew basics about the holocaust, and this lady lived through it. Like a lot of people, she had thought it was only Jews that were put into those camps. It made her think about how little she did know about the history of that war. She thought to herself, *"Why would she want me to help write her story?"*

Sara was lost in those thoughts until she heard Jill begin to speak again. "Sara, I have often used the phrase that I was 'old enough to remember, but young enough not to care.' In many ways it was a blessing that I was only six years old when the Germans came to the island. I guess that's where the 'young enough not to care' comes in. Being so young, I know I was spared much of the worry, anger, frustration, and a lot of the other emotions the adults were going through the whole time we were all under German control, and later in the camps in Germany. I of course, remember more in the later years near the end of the war. But much of the first couple of years when I was only six and seven years old, some of those memories have faded. There are times I will feel a certain way and wonder why.

"I'll think of something that I'm sure is a memory deep down that pops up at the time. I'll see in my mind snippets of memories. Like I said though, being as young as I was, probably is a blessing.

I have those snippets of memories, and later I got to hear the older people talking about things that happened, and then there was my own reading. I do know what happened in those first couple of years, and that helps fill in some of the blanks when one of those memories pop up.

We had a good life before the war. My father was a dentist on the island and had a successful practice. We lived a better life than many who lived on Guernsey at that time. My father had built our house. It was a beautiful home that he and my mother named Debonair." Jill stood and walked over to the table. She picked up a picture and walked over and handed it to Sara. It was a black and white picture of a stately house that to Sara even, looked very English. It was two stories and had what looked like a greenhouse on one end. Jill sat back down with a few other pictures in her hand she had picked up. Jill continued, "I remember more about the outside of the house really.

"Much more at this point than I remember the inside, but I do remember the inside was beautiful. I mostly remember the kitchen, and we had a large living room. Any time the weather was warm enough, my brother and I were outside.

"I suppose that's probably why I remember the outside of the house and grounds. I remember we had a detached garage and my father had one of the early Ford cars. I remember the greenhouse on the left side of the house in that picture. My father loved his garden. Many of those living on the island at that time were farmers.

"The most luscious tomatoes were one of the things Guernsey was known for. There were a lot of cattle on farms as well. You might not realize, but this is where Guernsey and Jersey cows originated. Many of the farmers weren't necessarily poor, but they did live a much simpler life I suppose than we did."

Sara handed the picture of the Debonair house back to Jill, and remarked, "I had always heard the terms Jersey and Guernsey cows but didn't know where the names came from. You must have had a different life growing up since your father wasn't a farmer.

"I mean your father being a dentist instead of a farmer." Jill exclaimed, "Most definitely. Again, as I said, many of those families who were farmers weren't poor, but we did enjoy a lifestyle that a good portion of those living on the island didn't have. We had the beautiful large home and yard. We also had a 35-foot motor cruiser named The Colleen. I wouldn't say it was a yacht, but that's what it seemed like to me as a six-year-old. My father would take us out in The Colleen on Sundays. I loved being on the water."

Jill handed Sara a couple more pictures. The pictures were of an older- looking boat that was quite large in Sara's mind. Sara thought, "Jill's friends on the island probably did consider it a yacht. Jill continued, "Growing up going out on the water in that boat, that's what gave me my love for boating that I just recently retired from. I captained my own boat that was a good size. I named it AME, and It was big enough to live on. It was a beautiful fifty-seven-foot Chris Craft." Jill handed Sara a couple more pictures.

Sara looked down at the picture of a large more modern boat and exclaimed, "Wow! this was your boat and you captained that yourself?"

Jill gave a light laugh and said, "Yes, it could have been quite intimidating for a lot of people, but I loved it and just went for it."

Olive and Stanley Pay, (Jill's parents, 1977)

Debonair, Jill's house before the occupation

Chapter 3:

Jill looked down at the picture of the Colleen and held it up again towards Sara saying, "There was an incident with The Colleen that gave us our first indication, or knowledge of how serious the war was becoming." Sara responded, "How so?" Jill held up her hand as if to pause for moment and then continued. "Before we get into that, tell me why you love history? Or as you said, used to." Sara thought for a moment, realizing this was probably the most engaging conversation she had with anyone since Robert's accident and especially since his death. She swallowed hard at that thought, fighting back the urge to start to cry. There was something special about this lady, Jill, that had given Sara a sense of calm and now a willingness to even hold a real conversation with someone.

Sara began, "I remember reading a story in 4th grade about Howard Carter who discovered the tomb of King Tut. I remember sitting there, imagining what he saw as he described looking through the hole they had made in the wall. He didn't know it at the time, but the hole opened into the main burial chamber.

"I have always remembered what he said when an assistant asked, "Can you see anything?" His response was, 'Yes! Wonderful things.' I remember thinking how cool it would be to discover something so historic. To be the first one to see something like that maybe in thousands of years. So that was my first time I thought that learning about history could really be fun. A lot of my friends, and I think most kids hate history class. They only memorize the names and dates for tests and then never give it another thought. But I've even thought about going into archeology. So that's pretty much it. It started with that short story about Howard Carter discovering the tomb."

Jill smiled as she remarked, "That's wonderful. I'm sure you would enjoy archeology. It can be a slow, arduous process, but how thrilling and exciting it would be, always being on the verge of possibly discovering something no one has seen for thousands of years. I guess it would be like a treasure hunt." Jill looked again at the picture she was holding of the family's boat The Colleen. She set it down on the coffee table, then stood up and walked over to a table against the wall. She opened a drawer to pull out a note pad and several pens. Jill walked back and sat down next to Sara.

She handed the note pad and pens to Sara before sitting back in her chair. Sara wondered what this was all about and looked at Jill questionably.

"Sara, if you are going to help me write this story, you are going to need to take some notes, right?" Sara looked down at the note pad and back up at Jill, stammering "Uh, yeah, I guess so." Sara briefly to herself that she hadn't really agreed to do this, but thought again, *"do I really have a choice? I guess I better make the best of it."* Sara took in a deep breath and then let it out saying, "Alright, I guess I don't really have a choice." She laughed a little under her breath and gave Jill a half smile before saying, "Right?" Jill smiled and said, "Well I surely can't make you do something you don't want to do, but if you're willing, Sara, I would really appreciate your help. Maybe between the two of us we can do it."

Jill picked up the picture of the family's boat again and handed it to Sara. "Sara, as I said a bit ago, the family boat, Colleen was involved in the first time we knew the war was getting serious and closer to home so to speak. My parents, along with my two older brothers, Paul and Roy were taking a little vacation.

"Their trip was on the Colleen. They left myself and my younger brother home with our nanny. I sometimes think I have a memory of being sad that I was missing out by not being able to go on the trip with them. They set out in the morning, setting sail for France. The Channel Islands are actually closer to France than they are to England.

"They first got to Cherbourg, then continued around the coast to Oistreham. After that they sailed on to Caen. I so wish I had been able to be on that trip. They continued up the River Seine to Paris. Paul later told how they moored the Colleen right by the Eiffel Tower, and when they got to the top of the Eiffel Tower, they could look down and see Colleen. I remember Paul saying how amazed he was at how small the boat looked from where they were at the top of the tower.

"Dad had hired a man to captain the boat named Mr. Bean. No, not the comedian." Jill chuckled a bit and continued. "Apparently, the captain was quite the drinker and father had to fire him while they were still on their trip. They sailed back down the Seine past several towns and past Le Havre. Le Havre is one of the towns that looks down on the D-Day beaches.

"Those beaches of course are where the massive invasion by the Allies took place in 1945 that began the liberation of France.

"My parents and brothers didn't realize that while they were cruising back to Cherbourg, war had been officially declared by Germany against France. They found out in short order that the Germans had already taken over several areas of France.

"When the family got to Cherbourg, they moored the boat and before they knew it, authorities ordered them off the boat and told my father it was being confiscated for the war effort. Whether Dad had a plan or not I'm not sure, but he told the officials that it was late, and they didn't have any place to stay. He asked if it was ok if they slept on the boat for just that night. I suppose things had not gotten so serious in France up to that point, so the military was perhaps a little more accommodating than they would be in a few short months.

The officials told Mom and Dad the family could sleep on the boat for just that night but would have to leave the boat immediately in the morning and gave them no indication where they were expected to go.

"I'm sure Mom was a little frantic about what was going to happen the next morning. After they got settled back on the boat and as nightfall came, Dad told Mom and the boys that they had to try and get away from France and try to get themselves and The Colleen back to Guernsey. After dark, Dad, Roy, and Paul kept a close eye on what was going on around the port. They watched for guards or security, particularly for any German guards. They figured other boats they saw moored around the same area had also been seized.

"Once it was completely dark, Dad told Mom to stay inside the cabin. Dad went to the stern while the boys aft, and they slowly and quietly untied the ropes that secured the boat to the dock. I'm sure everyone's hearts were beating a mile a minute. Dad went back to the boys and told them to keep watching, and when he gave the signal, they would push Colleen out beyond the jetties. Dad tapped on the railing to signal the boys. They all took one last look down the docks and pushed as hard as they could away from the dock. As they drifted out, their hearts were lodged up in their throats no doubt, and they kept looking back towards the docks and along the shoreline. They waited for someone to start shouting from the docks but heard nothing.

"Their greatest fear was that somebody would start shooting at them. That thought wasn't spoken by anyone, but they all knew very well it was a possibility they could be shot at. They were taking a huge chance because if they were caught, they didn't know what really would happen to them. Most likely, they would be thrown in jail, at least temporarily. With war having been declared, there was no telling what jail might be like.

"The tide was going out, and as they drifted further away from shore, they were relieved they had heard no shouts to stop. More importantly, they hadn't heard any gunfire. Dad told the boys when he thought they had gotten out far enough and told them to get inside. "He started the engine and they cruised slowly out of the harbor. They all held their breath, again waiting for some signs from the shore that they had been detected. Paul and Roy kept looking back towards Cherbourg until it was out of sight, making sure no one was coming after them.

"They were on their way and fortunately, no one was pursuing them. Had Dad not asked permission to stay the night on the boat and they had not gotten away,

"Mom, Dad, Paul, and Roy might very well have been stranded in France for the remainder of the war. The story of my early years would have been quite different, I suppose, if that had happened.

"They got back to Guernsey the next morning and shared their harrowing tale with everyone. There had been news regarding what Germany had been doing throughout Europe, but that was the first any of us knew it was reaching that close home. France was completely taken over by the Germans shortly after that. I remember Mom and Dad listening to news reports on the radio almost every night about what was going on. With the ease that the Germans took over France, it was obvious they had their sights set on England next. Of course, the Channel Islands sat between occupied France and the mainland of England. At its narrowest, it's only 21 miles across to England."

Jill sat back and sighed a bit, looking a little lost in her thoughts before smiling to Sara and saying, "I think we are done for today, my dear. Can I get you something to drink now?" Sara said she would like some water. Jill rose and walked into the kitchen. Sara was visually shaken a little by Jill's tale of the boat trip.

The trip, and the experience of her families escape from France. She had been so enthralled by the story she hadn't written any notes throughout the whole time Jill had been speaking. When Jill returned with the glass of water Sara asked if it would be ok if she took the note pad with her and she would write down some notes later. Jill sat down before saying, "Of course. I look forward to seeing you next Saturday." They both rose from their chairs and walked to the front door. Sara's mom was waiting outside in the driveway and Sara walked out without saying goodbye. Jill watched Sara walk to her mom's car and thought things had gone pretty well, all things considered.

Jill's family and friends aboard The Colleen in 1939

Jill's 57-foot yacht, The Ame

Chapter 4:

Sara was silent as she and her mom drove away. Susan finally broke the silence, "So how did it go? What did you do?" Sara was looking out the window and without looking over at her mother, said into the window "It was okay." "So, what did you actually do Sara? Sara gave a frustrated huff and breathed out hard as she remarked, "Nothing really." "Come on Sara, you had to do something. Come on, why don't you tell me." Sara jerked her head towards her mother and said in an angry tone, "Mom, don't start. I already said, I didn't do anything." Susan knew there was no sense in pushing the issue any further and said in an exasperated tone, "Alright! I'm sorry!"

When they got home, Sara went straight to her room. She sat on the edge of her bed and thought about the events of the day. Overall, it seemed kind of weird. She hadn't known what to expect as far as what she would be doing for her community service. She even imagined herself in one of those orange prison jumpsuits, picking up trash on the side of the road. She had been a little surprised and confused when they pulled into the Over-55 community.

Sitting on her bed now, she shrugged her shoulders and thought to herself, *it could be worse, that's for sure.*

Sara looked down at the notebook she had brought from Jill's and remembered she was supposed to write down some notes about what they had talked about that afternoon. She shook her head and said aloud to herself, "I don't get what this is all about, but well, I guess I'll make the best of it." She figured if nothing else, it was a distraction from the constant feelings of hate, anger, and depression she was constantly fighting within herself. She wasn't sure what she was really supposed to do ultimately but she began jotting down some notes.

At least part of her had to admit that she was curious about Jill's story. Sara of course had read stories about German camps. She never imagined she would actually talk to someone that had been forced to live in one, though. She wasn't even sure she had thought that anyone was still alive that had been in one of those camps. The time frame seemed like ancient history to her. After all, that was 80 years ago, she thought. She looked down at the page she had begun to write on.

The words she had written simply stated, "Jill, English, Island of Guernsey, good life, war." She saw the words "good life" and remembered what Jill had said about everything being taken away from her. Sara paused for a moment and then thought, *It was different for this lady than what I've gone through the last number of months since Robert's accident, and his...* She stopped in mid-thought, then her thoughts trailed off and she felt the tears welling up. She sat the notebook back down on the bed and laid her head down on her pillow. She closed her eyes and cried softly.

Sara didn't think much more during the rest of the weekend about Jill or the community service project, or work. She really didn't know just how to refer to what she was doing. Was it really work, she thought? The rest of the week was uneventful. Friday evening came and as they were sitting down to dinner, Susan remarked, "Don't forget, you have your community service tomorrow." Sara rolled her eyes and thought to herself, *"Oh gee mom, I would have forgotten all about it."* Paul laid his hand next to Sara's, saying, "Sara, can you tell us what you are doing for the community service work?" Sara thought, *this question is going to keep coming up so I might as well say something.*

Then maybe they will get off my back. Sara looked over at her father and stared for just a moment.

"Ok, fine. It's kind of weird really. All I know is I'm supposed to help this lady write her story about her life, or something like that." Susan and Paul both gave an interested look. Susan questioned, "Her life story? Is she a famous person or something?" Sara shook her head back and forth while saying, "Not that I know of, but all I did was sit the whole time I was there, and she talked. She showed me some pictures from when she was young. I figured, if this is what I am required to do, it could be a lot worse.

"That's it, really. I'm assuming tomorrow will be the same." Paul tilted his head and gave his daughter a crooked smile encouraged her by saying, "Well, like you said, it could be worse." Susan glanced over to her husband and gave him a slight smile. The conversation changed to other things for the remainder of the dinner.

Chapter 5:

The next morning Sara didn't complain or comment about her community service. Her mom didn't try to talk about it or anything else on the way to drop Sara off at Jill house. As soon as the car came to a stop in the driveway at Jill's home, Sara jumped out without saying anything. Susan leaned out the car window and yelled, "I love you!" Without turning around, Sara raised her hand that Susan sadly took as a dismissive gesture. As she backed out of the drive, she said out loud, "Please touch her heart, Lord."

Jill opened the front door as Sara walked up the steps to the porch. She greeted her with a smile saying, "Good morning. Sara, I've been looking forward to our time together today." Sara raised her eyes, looked at Jill and returned the greeting with, "Uh, yeah." Sara wasn't sure what made her think of it at that moment, but she thought to herself, *"Two years ago I would have been a lot more respectful to Jill's greeting."* Sara gave a slight shake of her head as if to clear those thoughts away, then nervously responded, "Hello."

Sara stepped into the house but stopped when she heard Jill say, "Hello, you must be Sara's mom."

Sara's eyes went wide, and she quickly turned around to see her mom standing in the doorway. She said in a frustrated tone, "Mom, it's not my first day of school. You don't have to walk me to the front door."

There was an awkward moment of silence, but Jill broke the tension saying, "I'm happy to meet your Mother Sara." Sara rolled her eyes and shook her head again as she turned and continued walking into the living room area. Jill extended her hand saying, "Hello there, I'm Jill." Susan introduced herself as she took Jill's hand, "I'm really happy that Sara is getting to work with you." Jill invited Susan in, but she responded, "Oh no, thank you, but maybe another time." Jill told her that she would like that. As Susan turned to go, she paused and turned back towards Jill and silently mouthed, "Thank you." Jill just smiled and nodded.

After Jill closed the door, she turned and saw Sara just standing in the middle of the room. "Why don't we sit at the table today for a while Sara if that's alright. That might be easier if you want to take some notes."

Sara shrugged her shoulders and walked over to the table and sat down. There were still some of the same photos laid out on the table just like the previous week, but Sara noticed a few news ones as well. Jill excused herself, saying she would be right back. When she returned, she had a pitcher on a tray with two glasses. As she sat down, she asked Sara if she would like some lemonade. One side of Sara's mouth turned up a little and she replied with a slight shrug, "OK".

As Jill filled the glasses, she reflected, "You know, not long after the Germans came to Guernsey, we would have given anything to have something like fresh lemonade, or a lot of other things." Sara thought, *ok, I guess we are going to dive right into It, then.* Jill began again, "I was only 6 when they first came, and took over our little island. I guess at that age I didn't really understand too much of what was happening. I do remember some things, and there are times I wonder if those memories are just other people's stories they have shared over the years. What happened to Mom and Dad and my brothers on The Colleen in France was our first taste of the war becoming real for us personally. June of 1940 was when it literally hit home.

"Several times, planes had flown over the island, and those planes were not British. One mistake our government had made in abandoning the islands - no one had told the Germans we no longer had any military there.

On June 28th that year, German planes attacked the St. Peter Port harbor. There was no reason for it, but later it was learned that they mistook farm trucks that were only loaded with tomatoes as military vehicles. Trucks were destroyed and many people were killed, and it was so unnecessary because our military had all already left the islands. Even though our home was a few miles away, I don't really know if I remember hearing the attack. The bombs really could be heard everywhere since the island is only about 9 miles long. It took another two days though, and on June 30th, German planes landed at the airport. That really began the occupation."

Sara sat there, not sure what to say. She managed to comment, "I've never heard anything about any of this." Jill said, "Well I guess after the war, no one thought much of it. With everything else that had happened all over Europe, it seemed insignificant.

"Sadly though, a lot of history is no longer taught to young people, including the part about the Germans occupation of the Islands.

"I love the fact that you as a young person are interested in history." Sara tried to suppress it, but she found herself smiling a little. Jills comment had made her feel positive about herself for the first time in a very long time. She just looked at Jill and nodded her head up and down in acknowledgement.

Jill continued, "Nevertheless though, it did not take too long before things began to change drastically. If you read much about it, the Germans wanted to make their occupation of the Islands a model for the rest of Great Britain. Their next goal was to take over England itself which was the last thing that stood really between them and total domination of all of Europe. They wanted the English people to believe that being occupied really wasn't all that bad. We were all supposed to go on with daily life as though nothing had changed."

Sara interrupted her at that point, saying, "I don't understand - if the Islands were part of England, why didn't they defend them?

"Wouldn't that have just emboldened the Germans to think the rest of England was going to be easy to take over?" Jill sighed and answered sadly, "There are several different arguments that those in charge made as to why they left all of us to basically fend for ourselves. It was as if we were never a part of England itself. There was a lot of animosity, but much of that didn't come out until later. As I said before, being so young, at my age I didn't understand or even care about most of that stuff. Some of my memories had to do with missing some of my friends who had evacuated before the occupation.

"The Germans wanted schools to continue, and they did. It wasn't too long, though, before even some of that changed because the Germans mandated that the students start learning German and for teachers to teach the German propaganda."

Jill had been looking away while she was talking, but she glanced back over at Sara and smiled when she saw Sara writing down some notes. Jill continued, "Like I said before, I was only six and didn't understand everything that was going on at first. I knew something bad and scary was happening, even at that age.

"I didn't fully understand why it all was happening though. The adults knew enough to be on edge. They had all started hearing stories from around town of things that were happening. It was confusing for me as a little girl to see the anxiety and worry on everyone's faces when adults would exchange hushed conversations.

"A real feeling of foreboding came just a few days later a German officer along with two armed soldiers came and knocked firmly on our front door. When my parents opened the door, they introduced themselves and acted polite, asking if they could come in. Of course, no one really had a choice to say no. My father stepped aside and motioned for them to come in.

"They started asking questions about the house and property. They asked who owned the house, how many bedrooms, etc. It wasn't long before their reason for being there became clear. In a tone that seemed as if we should all be honored that the German government should be showing interest in our home, the one who appeared to be in charge firmly stated, "We are requisitioning this house to be used for some of our officers.

"You will be required to vacate the premises by tomorrow. When we all heard that announcement, Mom's eyes went wide, and she started to say something I think but Dad put his hand on her arm to stop her. The officer said they appreciated my parents' cooperation, nodded towards my mother, then turned and walked out the door and were gone." Sara had stopped writing and her mouth hung opened in a little bit of surprise as she said, "They just kicked you out of your house? How could they do that?"

Jill laughed a little under her breath and said, "Well one of the first things the Germans did was confiscate all of the weapons on the island. So there really was no way to fight against anything they were doing. We were much more fortunate than most families because where my father's dental office was, my parents owned the apartment that was above the office. So, myself, my younger brother, and my parents moved out of the Debonair house into the apartment, bringing little more than some of our clothes. The Germans expected to have use of everything that was in the house, so all of the furniture and everything else had to stay. The only thing we would be allowed to take really was our clothes.

"The biggest disappointment at the time from my young perspective was I didn't have our wonderful yard to play in anymore."

Sara stated, "So you all had to move into a small apartment, then." Jill noticed a slight change in Sara's demeanor. Sara was becoming more engaging and seemed to be letting her guard down a little. Jill smiled, shook her head, and answered, "Yes, and it was pretty small and besides that, my grandmother was already living in the apartment. But again, we had it so much better than some people on the island. Most didn't have a second home or apartment they could go to.

"The Germans never asked people if they had another place to go to. It was just expected that when told do so, you would leave your home, and the Germans didn't care where you went from there, as long as you did as you were told. Most of the islanders pulled together, and there were sometimes several families moved in together in one house because they had no other place to go." Those were usually smaller houses already. So, they got kind of crowded with multiple families living in them. People did what they had to do though."

Sara shook her head back and forth before saying, "Well, you said your father had a car, at least you still had that to get around." Jill pursed her lips together, stifled a laugh and shook her own head back and forth as she followed with, "No, my dear, they took that away too." Sara gave another surprised look as Jill continued, "Once again, the Germans acted like we should be honored that the Third Reich would appropriate not only our home, but our car as well.

"They confiscated almost every car on the island. There were several businesses, and farm vehicles people were allowed to keep. That was only because the people who had those were expected to keep the markets and the occupation troops supplied with food and goods. I didn't go out much, but when we were outside, there were constantly German soldiers marching up and down the streets. I remember the loud clicking of their heels when they marched and especially when addressing a superior officer.

"To this day, I flinch when I hear a similar sound. It's funny how powerful your mind is and how just that simple sound can bring back memories.

"Memories of something that happened 80 years ago..."
Sara's eyes widened in surprise, and she couldn't help
but look away. She realized that this lady really did
have some understanding of what it was like, having
much of what you knew taken away, and there was
nothing you could do about it.

Chapter 6:

Jill picked up a book containing several pages of old black and white photos and opened it up. Sara looked down to see pictures of destroyed vehicles along the port. Jill pointed to one of the pictures saying, "This is what the area of the port looked like after they bombed it and gunned people down with their machine guns as they were trying to run away. I've read that the Guernsey bailiff complained to the German commandant about being expected to cooperate. He pointed out to the commandant they had bombed the island and killed people for no reason. The response was, "Your government should have made it clear they had left the island unprotected; therefore, they are defenseless."

Sara studied the picture of the destruction on the port. She felt a chill come over her as she saw what looked like bodies or maybe even pieces of bodies among the destruction. She closed her eyes as the horrible scenes from the movie, Saving Private Ryan played out in her mind.

Jill pointed to a few other pictures showing German soldiers on the streets.

Sara pointed to a picture of a German soldier standing next to a British policeman in conversation. She asked, "Why is there a policeman just standing there casually talking to a German soldier?" Jill responded, "Well, like I said, they expected things to continue as though nothing had changed. So, at first, most businesses could continue operating and the German authorities expected the local government to keep things in order, including the local policing. I should correct one thing. When I said most business could continue, all but the Jewish-owned businesses could continue operating.

Most of the Jewish people had evacuated to the mainland before the Germans came. They knew what lay ahead for them based on reports coming out of Poland, France, and especially Germany itself. Everything was under German control and authority now, so the reality was nothing continued as normal anymore. The Germans demanded that Guernsey still police itself and expected the local government to cooperate fully and to keep the citizens in order. So, in the end, we still had our policemen around town, but they really were under German control" Sara interrupted, saying, "What did the Jewish people do with their property and their businesses?"

Jill had a somber look, pausing a moment before speaking. "Some left, even giving away their businesses to other people that were staying on the island. Many didn't know if they would ever be back, and they just left with whatever they could carry along with them." Sara felt the lump in her throat return, and just shook her head. Reading about many of these events was one thing, but to hear directly from someone who had experienced them first-hand made it not just more real, but more disturbing.

Vehicles destroyed after German bombing raid at the port on Guernsey. 34 people were killed and another 33 injured.

Jill continued, "The lucky ones, they had bicycles for getting around. It didn't take long, though, for parts to run out for things like tires and innertubes for people's bikes. Eventually, people did whatever they could to keep using their bikes, like wrapping pieces of rope around the rim after their tires completely fell apart. You could hear bikes bouncing and rattling down the streets because they didn't have tires on them anymore.

"I think the hardest thing for most of our parents was they had no idea how long this all would last. I think people had faith that eventually the Germans would be defeated. However, we were basically cut off from what was happening in the rest of the country, or even what was really happening in all of Europe. The only ones who knew anything were those who had radios and could still listen to some news on the BBC. It wasn't long, though, before a notice came out that everyone was to turn in any, and all radios they owned."

"You weren't even allowed to have a radio?" Sara said incredulously. Jill shook her head and saying, "No, and in fact later, people went to jail if they were caught with one.

"Some people had hidden them when the order had come to turn them in.

"One of the hardest things for some people to understand later was that fellow citizens would report to the Germans about neighbors hiding a radio." Sara gave another one of her surprised looks that had become common suddenly and blurted out, "Wait! Why would people turn in their neighbors like that?" Jill pressed her lips together with a grieved look on her face answered Sara's question.

"Sara, unfortunately something like war brings out the worst in some people. Some thought they would gain favor with the Germans if they did things like report people for violating some of the rules. The sad fact is it worked in many cases. It eventually was known, for people who cooperated like that, the authorities would turn the other way when those people did something wrong. Their infractions were overlooked since they were helping the Germans keep control. That's what it was all about - control."

Chapter 7:

Jill was pleased when she saw Sara writing things down in the notebook that she had given Sara the previous week. At one point, Sara stopped writing, looked at Jill before saying, "So, I still don't understand how you ended up in a German concentration camp." "Well, my dear, that actually happened a little more than two years after the Germans first took over the islands."

Sara looked surprised as she asked her next question. "Were the people on the island starting to fight against the Germans and that's why?" Jill shook her head as she answered, "That wasn't the reason, and I didn't realize all that was going on because how old I was at the time, but there was resistance by some. That upset others on the island because each time there was an incident, the restrictions were tightened. It didn't take long before basic food products were getting harder and harder to find, and that just made tensions among everyone even worse.

"It wasn't really until after that more things came out into the open and people realized that the Germans never planned on deporting any of the islanders.

"At least not families and children like they eventually did. Before the mass deportations that my family were part of, there were more than 500 people from Guernsey and the other islands that were either imprisoned in different places or sent to German camps because they committed some type of offense. Some of those that were imprisoned were done so just for having a radio like I said, or for some other minor offense...and some of those, sadly died in those prisons."

Jill looked down and shook her head, then more to herself than to Sara she said softly, "Man's inhumanity to man." She looked over at Sara and saw that Sara had stopped writing and was just looking down at the pen she was still holding against the notebook. Sara looked up and in a soft voice asked, "Can we take a break?" Jill smiled. "Sara, I think that's a good idea, how about some lunch?"

Jill went into the kitchen but continued talking. She began asking Sara about her love of history. She called from the kitchen asking what parts of history, or time periods she was most interested in. "Well to be honest, I had started getting interested in the early wars.

"Earlier than the World Wars. The ones I've studied the most are the Revolutionary War and Civil War. I hadn't had that much interest in the later wars. Now though, I'm seeing there's a lot more to all the stories really." Sara thought for a moment, then smiled before continuing,

"You know, my brother Robert......." As her voice trailed off the smile faded quickly, but she took a deep breath and continued. "My brother Robert liked history and I'm sure that's part of the reason I got interested in it." Her lips tightened a little, but then she gave a slight smile again as she realized this was the first time that she had a smile on her face when thinking about anything relating to Robert in a long time.

Jill wanted to tread lightly when it came to talking about Sara's brother. She had walked back to where she could see Sara from the kitchen. She liked seeing Sara smile a little after mentioning him. Jill leaned against the door frame and remarked, "I bet your brother would be really proud of you." Sara didn't know Jill was looking at her. She looked up, a bit surprised, and one corner of her mouth turned up a little with an attempt at a smile.

Sara was silent after that and she choked up a little, but it was one of the first times she didn't break down in tears when uttering his name or thinking about him. She raised her head, and with a quiet voice and a slight smile said to Jill, "Thank you." Jill silently acknowledged Sara, then turned and went back into the kitchen.

Sara got up from her chair and wandered into the kitchen to see what Jill was making. "That smells good; what is it?" Jill smiled. "Well, my dear, it's one of my favorite things to make for lunch. You'll probably think it's a little strange, but it's a very British thing. Baked beans on toast." Sara gave that scrunched nose and eyebrow look again as she repeated, "Baked beans on toast? That is strange." Sara immediately followed her remark with, "Oh, I'm sorry I shouldn't have said that." Jill laughed and waved her hand towards Sara to let her know she took no offense.

Jill looked at Sara, saying, "It's funny - sometimes when you had things too often growing up, you never want to eat them again, but I still like this. After the war when we eventually went to England to live, there was rationing of most things for another nine years."

Sara gave a shocked look as she exclaimed, "Nine years! Why nine years? Jill shook her head as she continued, "You have to understand that much of England had been decimated. London especially was a mess. It took years and help from a lot of other countries to rebuild not only England, but much of Europe. The United States and Canada were two of the main sources of help.

"The U.S. and Canada sacrificed a lot during the war to help liberate England and the rest of Europe. Both countries helped supply us with milk, meat, vegetables, and other supplies. Food especially was rationed, so most of our food was simple, like beans on toast." She smiled and looked over at Sara saying, "I still love it, though. Beans with breakfast is pretty much a staple in England. That, and a half-roasted or grilled tomato, too." Sara wrinkled her nose and thought aloud, "Really? For breakfast?" Jill gave a chuckle as she answered Sara with, "Yep, for breakfast. Beans were one of the things we always got with the food rations, but Brits liked baked beans before the war, too." Jill served up two plates of toast and baked beans, and then walked in and sat them on the table where the pictures had been moved over to the side.

Sara sat down while Jill refilled their glasses from the pitcher of lemonade.

Jill casually spoke, "So, Sara, tell me about your parents." Sara's eyebrows narrowed together in a quizzical look and in a cautious tone asked, "My parents? Why do you want to know about my parents?" Jill laughed a bit and answered, "oh, I was just curious, and one thing I was wondering whether your love of history comes from them."

Sara nodded, "Oh, well I guess so. Dad is always talking about needing to know our country's history. I know they are serious about keeping informed, knowing what's going on, and always are stressing to us about how important it is to vote once we are old enough. My dad is pretty involved in a couple of organizations that promote history education. He has researched enough that he was accepted into the Sons of the American Revolution. You need to have a direct ancestor who fought in the Revolution to be accepted into that. I think Dad's ancestor is something like his sixth-generation great-grandfather. He was killed in the Revolutionary War. My Mom and Dad both do a lot with genealogy. I guess that's history too."

Jill nodded, "Genealogy and family heritage is most definitely history. My own family has quite the history that contained a few surprises along the way. I'm sure most family's histories have some twists and turns. I know mine sure did, but it is what it is, and it's good to know the whole story.

"It helps you understand a lot about yourself, and probably helps you deal with certain things in your life when you understand where you came from. I'm sorry, I'm just rambling. I would like to meet your parents at some point, but that's not important right now."

Chapter 8:

Sara took a few bites of the beans and toast, smiled and remarked, "Hey! This is actually pretty good." Smiling to herself, she said under her breath, "Who'd a thunk?" The very next moment, Jill noticed Sara's expression change. Sara sat her fork down, her head and shoulders drooped, and she willed herself not to cry. She composed herself, then looked at Jill, "I'm sorry, that 'Who'd a thunk' was one of Robert's favorite expressions and I said it without thinking." Jill reached across the table and placed her hand gently on top of Sara's. "My dear, don't be ashamed or embarrassed; you're honoring your brother by using one of his favorite sayings. Would you tell me a little about your brother?" Sara looked up with her eyes widened somewhat, paused momentarily, then decided to go ahead and take the plunge into a conversation she had not been willing to have with anyone for nearly two years.

"Before the...before everything happened, he was my best friend. I guess I need to stop thinking about what happened after his accident because that's not how I want to remember him.

"Before the accident, I could talk to him about things I couldn't talk to my parents about. No matter what I was going through, he always knew when something was wrong. He would come into my room and recognize a particular look on my face. He would sit down, put his arm around my shoulder and say, "Alright dork, spill the beans. What's up?" He came to all my sporting events. I would look around the gym or wherever I was, and then I'd see this handsome, broad-shouldered young man. Then he would smile and always give me two thumbs-up. That always encouraged me or gave me the boost I needed to go on."

Jill reached across the table and put her hand on Sara's again. Jill smiled, saying, "Sounds like he was a pretty special guy, and I bet he's proud of you." Sara sat for a bit, not saying anything. She finally looked up at Jill and she gave a couple of quick nods saying, "I really want him to be, but....... I haven't really done anything in a while to make him proud of me." Jill slapped her hand down on the table, startling Sara a little, and declaring, "Well my dear, maybe helping me is the first step." With that, Jill pushed her chair back and told Sara, "Wait right here, I want to show you something."

Sara took a deep breath and thought to herself, *I can't believe I got through talking about Robert without bawling like a little girl.* She wiped away the beginning of a tear, yet she found herself smiling a bit. She felt a feeling of warmth in her chest she hadn't felt in a long time.

Jill came back into the room carrying a small box. She had gone to get the box because she thought it was a good time to change the subject. She sat down and slowly opened the box, taking out a folded piece of paper. She gently unfolded it to lay out on the table. Sara looked down at the picture of what appeared to be a needle point on a piece of burlap material. Jill said, "We'll get to more of the story of when my family got sent to Germany, but first, I wanted to show you this. I made this when I was probably about ten years old while we were living in the camp in Biberach, Germany. They call something like this a sampler."

"Wow!" Sara Said, "You were only 10? That's beautiful. Do you not have the actual piece anymore?" Jill smiled appreciatively, answering, "Thank you. My youngest son wanted the sampler, so I had given it to him.

"I was going to send it to the War Museum in Guernsey, but my son doesn't want to give it up. I'm glad it's special to him though, and that it will stay a part of my family." Jill folded the print again and put it back in the box. She sat it aside saying, "Ok, ready to work some more?"

Jill picked up their plates and took them into the kitchen. She came back in the room and sat down. "Well, so how was your first English lunch Sara?" "Well, I have to admit I thought it was kind of weird when you first told me what we were having, but I liked it." "I'm not as English as some who really stick to a lot of traditions and even their speech. I love my country, but I'm more American now than anything." Jill said smiling.

Jill continued, "Okay, so where did you stop in your notes?" Sara picked up her notebook and scanned down the page. "You told me about restrictions getting worse because of people resisting more and more." Jill replied, "Oh yes. Well, the Germans wanted to make the occupation of the Islands a propaganda tool. It never really worked.

"But the purpose of the propaganda was to wear down the British support of the war, and at the same time, increase sympathy toward Germany.

I think the Germans thought if they could somehow show the people in England that being occupied really wasn't all that bad then that is when the support for the war by the British citizens would start to wane. They figured, then, everyone would pressure the government to just accept that it was inevitable that the Germans would take over.

"So, they should just make the best of it. So, I'm sure it was frustrating to those Germans in charge that some were causing problems and making it more difficult for them. They were under a lot of pressure from Berlin to make the occupation of Guernsey and the other islands work well. Or at least appear to do so.

"Much of this part of the story I learned later. I was still only six years old when the Germans first came onto the island. As I've said, I only have bits and pieces of memories from the first year. I've said, too, that was a mixed blessing. Older kids, especially some of the teenage boys, got into a lot of trouble. Some were caught doing different things and they were put in prison.

"They went away for anywhere from a month or two to even longer. Teenagers were caught stealing things from German guards or store houses. Some threw rocks at Germans in the streets and sometimes they were caught painting anti-German graffiti on rocks or buildings. The Germans demanded respect, while still expecting everyone to just carry on with the government-sponsored charade. We would hear from time to time about someone having been taken away for trivial reasons.

"Probably the biggest change for a lot of people was when food started becoming more and more scarce. It didn't take long before things like coffee, sugar, salt, and fresh meat became more difficult to get. Vegetables were still plentiful at first, and that became many people's only diet. We were more fortunate though. My father's business had been successful, and our family had money. That's one thing the Germans didn't confiscate.

"A black market was soon established from what I've read, and I don't know if my mother and father bought things through the black market or not, but I imagine they would have.

"Things got much more difficult for those still on the island in the latter years, but of course, as I said, we weren't there. Myself and my family spent the last three years in the German camps.

"If you go to Guernsey today, you'll see museums and memorials, memorials of those who died in the resistance. As I mentioned, some people went to prison after getting caught for the mere offense of listening to a radio. Some died while in prison because of acts of abuse done to them, or starvation due to lack of food, or because they were denied medical attention. Some of the memorials are for those who died while in different prisons.

"If their sentence was more than about three months, instead of being put into the local prison in Guernsey, they were sent to much harsher prisons in France and some on to prisons or camps in Germany to serve out their sentences. Some of those never returned. I truly am thankful that I was not old enough to remember many of the horrors from the entire five years of the war. I often wish I didn't remember as much as I do. They never mentioned it, so, I never knew if my parents ever thought we might not get out of Germany alive.

"I know I still have scars, and everything that happened affected the rest of my life, but many people and families suffered far more than ours did. Even so, I would not wish on anyone what our family went through.

Chapter 9:

Sara spent time in her room that evening before dinner, going through the notes she had taken, and thinking back on what Jill had shared. Eventually her mom called her for dinner. She sat at dinner, still thinking about some of the things that Jill had told her, and as she sat there, Sara thought, *"She hasn't even gotten to the really bad stuff yet."* Paul and Susan had noticed Sara's mood and were afraid she was drifting back to where she had been just a few weeks before, lost in deep depression. They thought she had been improving, but now they were not so sure. Paul cautiously ventured, "So, how did things go today with Jill, the lady you are working with? That's her name, right?" Sara just held her fork, staring off to the side. Without looking at her father she quietly remarked, "It, it was ok." Susan noticed the thoughtful look on her daughters' face, and when Paul started to press for more of an answer, she reached over and put her hand on his. He looked at Susan and she smiled, shaking her head back and forth slightly, to say, "It's ok."

There was a tenderness between Susan and Paul that had not been present for a long time.

Paul thought that perhaps some real healing had started taking place, especially in Susan. He hoped and prayed the same was happening for Sara, no matter how small it might be, any steps forward were further along than their family had been in a very long time.

Sara finally turned to look at her parents and commented, "You know, the world can be a really cruel place sometimes." Paul and Susan weren't exactly sure what to make of Sara's statement. Paul had a quizzical look on his face and said to Sara, "Is there something specific that makes you say that?" Sara sat just looking down at her plate that was still half-full, saying nothing for a bit. She finally in a frustrated voice answered her father saying, "I just think it can be a really cruel place. I think I'm finished." Susan and Paul both looked at each other a little wide-eyed and concerned at what she meant. Susan said in a pleading tone with her voice breaking as she spoke, "Sara, please don't give up." Sara eyes squinted together, then she realized what they were thinking. She raised her head to look at her mother and said, "Give up? Oh, no, I'm sorry, I meant I'm finished with my dinner. I think I'm going to go up to my room. With that, she got up from her chair and left the room.

Paul and Susan just looked at each other, neither one knowing what to think or say. Paul finally turned to Susan saying, "I think if it's ok with the court, that it might be a good idea if we talked to this Jill person. If we do that, then we can understand maybe a little more about what's going on in Sara's mind right now."

After Sara went up to her room, she sat at her small desk organizing and adding to the notes she had taken. She made a footnote, "Talked about Robert today without crying. Didn't think I would ever do that again." After she wrote those words, she sat with her eyes closed. She started thinking about Robert and knew that if he were still alive, he would be sitting across from her on the bed giving her advice. He might be teasing her, but that was one of his ways of breaking down her walls so she could look at a situation more clearly. That always brought a smile to her face, and then he'd give her a huge smile in return along with that big "thumbs-up" sign. She felt a tear roll down her cheek, but she noticed that she didn't really feel sad this time. Instead, she felt a sense of peace she hadn't felt in a long time. She thought to herself, *Wow! The second time today talking or thinking about Robert, and I'm not feeling angry.*

A few days later, Paul and Susan went to the court and asked if they could speak to the judge that had presided over Sara's case. Judge Montgomery welcomed them graciously to his office. After they sat down, Paul was the first to speak. "I know you are a busy man, Judge, so I'll get to the point of why we wanted to see you." Judge Montgomery held up his hand and shook his head back and forth slightly as he said, "Please, no worries, the main thing is that we're trying to help Sara. So, are you having some concerns about how she's doing with her community service?"

Susan spoke up saying, "Not really concerns, specifically, it's just we really don't know what it is she's actually doing. There are times when Sara comes home after spending the day with this lady Jill, and she seems depressed. Other times she seems almost like her old self, even smiling some and engaging in a conversation." Judge Montgomery smiled saying, "Well, I think maybe that's a good sign." Paul remarked, "I'm not sure what you mean. It's hard seeing her come home the times when she seems more depressed, and we don't know what happened during that day to put her in the mood she is in. We have no real clue what this community service is all about."

Judge Montgomery folded his hands together as he shook his head back and forth saying, "You know, I think I owe you both an apology. I should have taken you both aside and explained what Sara's community service was going to entail. At the end of her case when I handed down the penalties, I wanted some time to think about what type of community service would best help Sara.

"When multiple young people are involved in whatever resulted in them standing before me in my courtroom, I still try to look at each one individually and assess what is going to help each one. My goal is always to help them not become another statistic. It doesn't always work, but I never want to think a young person is a lost cause. I can't go into details, but some of the girls Sara was with the night they broke into the town museum... Well, let's just say that they already had a previous history with the courts. Some offenses more serious than others. So, I might have dealt with them much different. That's all I will say regarding the other girls. I looked at Sara's profile, so to speak, and I read the letter that you as her parents had submitted to the court. So, I knew a little about Sara, and that is why I chose the course of action I did in her case.

"We aren't trying to hide anything, but I would ask that you trust me on this. I believe Sara working with Jill is going to help her. What Sara and your family has been through, there isn't an overnight fix to all those emotional wounds. As you know yourselves, you never forget."

Susan nodded saying, "Well, I can say this, there are at least times when Sara has started to show signs of her old self. That at least is encouraging. So maybe you're right, what she is doing with Jill is helping. As her mom, I just want to fix her." Judge Montgomery consoled Susan saying, "I can most definitely understand that. Let's give it some time." Paul asked, "Can you at least tell us what she's actually doing?" The judge continued, "I read about Sara's love of history, or at least how much she used to love history. Jill has a very interesting life story, and her family has asked her for years to write about it. So, Sara's time with Jill, her assignment, or community service is to basically help Jill write her memoirs and tell her story." Paul simply commented, nodding his head, "Interesting!" He was wondering within his mind what might be so fascinating about this woman Jill's life to want to actually write about it.

They thanked Judge Montgomery and told him they would do their best to be patient. They left feeling a little better now that they knew what Sara was doing after they dropped her off each Saturday.

Chapter 10:

Sara sat across from Jill at the table the following Saturday morning. Jill asked if she had any questions or thoughts about what they had talked about so far. Sara said, "Well I have a lot of questions, but most of them are about things that probably happened later. I mean things later than what you have been talking about so far. I guess you'll share those things and probably answer a lot of those questions eventually anyway. Mainly I have questions about your time in Germany."

Jill sat silent for a moment, then nodded her head and said softly, "You know, I still have questions myself. I have purposely not thought much about those days very often. When I do, though, some of my questions are simply the 'why' and 'how' questions." Sara interrupted her saying, "I don't understand. What do you mean 'why and how'?" Jill again remained silent for a moment and Sara thought maybe she was pressing too much about things that were too hard for Jill to think about or share. Sara said apologetically, "I'm sorry, I shouldn't have..." Jill held up her hand to motion for Sara to stop.

Jill shook her head back and forth saying, "Oh no, please don't apologize. I knew going into this that a lot of it would be hard. I'm the one that said let's do this, and I am determined to get it done. Besides that, it was me that asked you if you had any questions." Jill smiled, patted Sara's hand across the table as she said reassuringly, "It will help me if I can keep things in the order they happened, and I do remember, but don't hesitate to ask anything. I might answer the question down the road a bit if that's okay." Sara answered again in an apologetic tone, "Oh, absolutely. I'm pretty sure I understand why some of this is hard for you.

She continued, "Ok, you said your questions sometimes are the why and how questions. Can you tell me what you meant?" Jill's head tilted slightly, and her gaze went a little to the side. After an awkward moment of silence, she spoke. "Why did all of this have to happen at all? Why my family, why me? Why did some people die that my family probably knew, but we came through it alive? Then there are the how's. How could sane, reasonable people allow this to happen? How could people do what they did to other human beings? Horrible things. At some point you realize what happened was not done by sane, or reasonable people.

"You end up just shaking your head because there are no good answers."

Jill stopped speaking and looked down at her hands linked together. Sara sat watching Jill look down at the table for a bit and then said, "You know what? I think you are one of the bravest people I've ever met." Jill looked up and gave a small laugh under her breath, saying, "Why would you say that? I'm just a regular person like everyone else." It was Sara's turn to shake her head back and forth, as she exclaimed, "Are you kidding me? What you and your family went through, there's not a whole lot of people or families that have experienced anything like that, and I haven't even heard the rest of your story. I have a feeling it gets much worse."

Jill smiled, reached across and put her hand on top of Sara's to counter, "Well, there are more than six million Jews and their families that would disagree about not many others going through anything like that. I know what you are saying though, and I appreciate it. I don't consider myself brave. I was a little girl. In a lot of ways, I was just along for the ride. It wasn't for me like it was for my parents and the other adults.

"I'm sure they were constantly worrying about what the next day would bring."

She paused for a moment and then continued. "Can you imagine that Sara, wondering every single day, living in fear of what might happen tomorrow? Not just wondering what you were going to be doing the next day but imagining if your family or your children might even be alive by the end of the next day. I'm sure many asked themselves a lot of those types of questions. Questions like, would you hear about a friend that got shot by a German soldier the day before? Would you or your children be taken away somewhere? If you were taken away, where would they take you, what would happen, and would you ever come back. I'll keep saying it, I was blessed to have not been older during all of it so that I don't remember any more than I do. There are plenty who have far worse scars than I have, but I remember enough, and honestly, that's too much."

Jill paused again, looking towards the wall, not really focusing on nothing in particular. She turned finally and looked at Sara again. "I have never talked this much about that time in my life, not even with my family.

"So, forgive me when I stop sometimes and just, I don't know, I guess when I stop and just think." Sara felt like she ought to say something, but Jill held her hand up slightly and smiled.

Jill continued, "It's ok. This is good for me I suppose and there are those in my family, especially some of the younger ones that have begged me to tell them more of the details about those times." Sara smiled and said, "Well I can understand them wanting to know. I would always be asking you too. You asked if I could imagine some of those things you mentioned. I don't think anyone really can if they didn't live through it themselves. I guess what you said earlier about not telling somebody they know how the other person feels if they really don't. I do understand that better now. You really can't do that unless you lived it, too."

Jill nodded without saying anything more. She reached and took another sip from her glass. and sat it down. With a more determined look now, she continued, "Well, I know it is important for young people especially. They need to know this part of our history. I don't mean just British history, but history in general.

"That war and those times affected almost the entire world. Let me ask you a question, and it's ok if you don't know the answer, it's just a question." Sara said in reply, "Sure, go ahead," Sara invited. Jill nodded and asked, "Do you know how many people died in all of WWII?" Sara put her pen down and folded her hands under her chin, resting her elbows on the table to think for a moment. She finally answered, "I'm not really sure. I guess what most people heard or remember hearing is something like five million Jews died. I know a lot more people than that did, just from the fighting I guess, not just the Holocaust."

Sara saw what was either a serious or maybe a sad look come over Jill's face. There was an uncomfortably long pause while she waited for Jill to say something. She wondered if a memory might have surfaced that she probably had never wanted to relive. Sara wanted to say something more, but she didn't know what, so she just waited.

The pause lasted only about 10 seconds, but as Sara sat there waiting and not knowing what to say, it seemed like a full minute of uncomfortable silence. Jill slowly shook her head back and forth.

"Sara, the actual estimate is that over 75 million people died during that war." Sara's eyes went wide as she gave Jill an astonished look. Sara shook her head, and in a louder tone that she intended said questioningly, "75 million! Are you serious? That can't be true. That would be like an entire population of a country being completely wiped out." Jill nodded her head in response.

"You're right. So, think about it this way - that's twice the entire population of Canada today. "That would be as if nearly a fourth of all the people in the United States suddenly were gone right now.

"That number hits home for myself when I realize, it's actually more than the entire population of England. It really would be like that for most countries in the world. There would be no more people left. Everyone, just gone. It's been almost eighty years since the war ended, and a lot of people don't understand how bad it was and what really was at stake. If the Germans and the Japanese had not been defeated, the world would be a vastly different place today."

Chapter 11:

Sara watched Jill's expression when she finished talking. Jill had closed her eyes and taken in a long, deep breath. Sara could only imagine that Jill was picturing in her mind what might have happened if the outcome of the war had been different. Sara thought again that Jill hadn't even gotten to any of the truly ugly parts of her story. What she saw and experienced perhaps during her time in the German camps and probably even before. A thought came to Sara's mind, and she wondered, *had Jill ever thought about how much longer she and her family would have survived that ordeal?* Sara thought in all likelihood if the Germans had prevailed or even hung on for much longer, they would have simply let people starve or just worked more of them to death.

Sara sat there silent, not really knowing what to say or what her next question might be. Jill finally commented, "Well, let's get back to what did happen, okay?" Sara nodded and looked back down at her notes. She said, "Well, you had asked if I had any questions so far, and I said my questions were about the later stuff. About the camps in Germany."

Jill nodded while saying, "Well, it was two years before we were sent to Germany. A lot happened even in those first two years.

I was 8 years old at the end of the first two years of the occupation of Guernsey, so as each year went by, I was old enough to remember more things. Like I said previously, some of those earlier years are just snippets of memories. Different ones pop up now and then, though. After the Germans first arrived, it seemed like more soldiers arrived every day. I don't remember it so much, but I know they would march through the streets in their formations all the time. They almost always were carrying their guns. Not just soldiers were arriving, but equipment, military-type vehicles, and really what can only be described as slave laborers."

Sara stopped writing and tilted her head with a questioning look to comment, "Slave laborers, I don't understand." With a very somber look, Jill continued, "Prisoners that the Germans forced to work. They were prisoners from other countries the Germans had already taken over or captured in different battles. A lot of them were Russian and Polish, but they included a few other countries too.

"The Germans set up camps on other islands and almost immediately started building fortresses along the harbors and on the hills above the coastline. They were always worried that Great Britain was going to attack the Islands and try to take them back. So, they placed land mines all along the beaches and hillsides. More than once I'm sure, a farmer or child just trying to find some food or get down to the beach to get some fish or clams was injured or killed by the mines.

"Those laborers though, the prisoners, hundreds of those prisoners died there on the Islands. Either from untreated disease, starvation, or literally worked to death is the only way to describe it. There were Jews that were brought to the Islands from other countries, especially Germany. They were basically slave laborers too. The Germans required the local officials to identify those Jews that remained on the Islands before the occupation. Their IDs were marked with a large J.

"The whole issue of the few Jewish people who remained on the Islands is another horrible part of our British history. There was only a small number of Jews that remained in Guernsey, and that primarily was because they weren't British-born Jews.

"Because of that, Great Britain would not accept foreign-born passports as valid entry into Great Britain. So, those Jewish people were forced to stay instead of evacuating before the Germans arrived. The head of our local government, he turned them over to the Germans eventually for deportation. A few were at first just deported over to France to the port city of Saint Malo. Historical records showed that a few of those Jews ended up in the same camp where our family was sent. The three that were sent to Saint Malo, they were rounded up not too long after settling there and were sent to the infamous Auschwitz concentration camp where they all died."

Sara noticed again that Jill had paused, her head had dropped a little and she had grown more contemplative. She looked at Sara but didn't immediately say anything. Sara waited. Jill stared down at the table, and finally looked up. "The truth is, unfortunately the British government basically sentenced those Jews to death who remained on the Islands. By not allowing them to evacuate to the mainland, they were surely doomed." Jill swallowed hard. Sara felt as if she might start crying herself if Jill started, and she didn't even know why. She just knew she would.

Jill eventually continued. "I've said before - as bad as my family's experience was, some had it far worse. If you know any history about that time, just the mention of the word Auschwitz sends a shiver down your spine. You can't even see the word or hear it without remembering that over 1,000,000 Jews were murdered in just that one concentration camp."

Jill's countenance changed at the mention of that number "A lot of them were just children." Sara closed her eyes as if to try and wipe from her mind the picture that Jill had painted for her with those words. She felt that sensation down her spine that Jill had mentioned. Sara tried to speak, saying, "I can't, ...a million, I..." Jill reached across, placed her hand on top of Sara's again saying, "I'm sorry, I didn't mean to upset you." Sara looked at Jill and slowly shook her head back and forth. "No, please Jill, it's ok. That number is hard to even comprehend" Sara's voice trailed off as she finished with, "Even though I know it's true." They both sat in silence for a moment, overcome with emotion.

Sara was the first to speak, "I was just thinking about the genealogy stuff.

"The stuff my parents are really into and working on. I thought about all of the soldiers and prisoners, people that were murdered and the millions of Jewish people you mentioned before, their personal family histories stopped right in their tracks. They didn't get to continue raising their children, or see their grandchildren be born. Some never even got to have children. Some probably even saw their own children murdered in front of them."

The thought of what she had just said brought a lump to her throat. Sara drew her lips in and pressed them tight against each other, fighting back wanting to just burst out in tears. A single tear slowly rolled down one side of Sara's face and she reached her hand up to wipe it away. Jill squeezed Sara's hand lightly and said, "I think there are ways many of them do carry on. I like to think in some ways, sometimes, they might speak through other people." They both sat in silence again for a moment. Jill pulled her hand back saying, "Oh My, listen to me, I'm being pretty silly. I would say that's enough for today, what do you think? Sara regained her composure and nodded her head without saying anything.

Jill smiled, "I made some sweet bread Sara. Why don't we have some for a little snack."

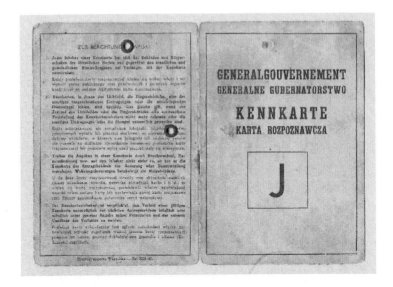

Mandatory Jewish ID card required

German officers supervising forced laborers

Chapter 12:

Sara and her family attended church the next morning as they almost always did. After the service Sara said to her mom, "I'm going to walk over to the cemetery; I'll be home a little later." Susan said excitedly, "Oh, I can go with you and drive. You don't have to walk." Sara shook her and smiled, "Thanks Mom, but I'd rather go by myself if it's ok." Susan couldn't conceal her worried expression, and Sara picked up on it immediately. Sara put her hand on her mother's arm, "It's ok, Mom, I'll be alright." Susan smiled and then sighed a little. "Ok, honey, don't be gone too long." As Sara walked away, Susan called out, "Sara! I can come pick you up in a little while, so you don't have to walk." Sara turned to look at her mom without stopping and said in an elevated tone, "Mom!"

Sara arrived at the entrance to the cemetery and stopped for a moment. She looked across the acres of headstones and thought back to what Jill had said about all the people who had died as a result of WWII. As she made her way towards Robert's grave, she noticed really for the first time those grave markers that had symbols or markers honoring the person as a veteran.

She stopped in her tracks when she noticed a headstone with a Jewish star. She stared at the symbol for a moment and felt that same shiver run up her spine again. As the sensation she felt subsided, she continued walking.

Sara stood in front of Robert's grave for several minutes before sitting down on the bench facing the headstone. She looked down for a bit and saw an ant pushing and pulling on a dead beetle that was probably ten times the size of the ant. She was fascinated watching the ant because it simply refused to give up. She said outloud, "I think you might have bitten off a little more than you can chew, little fellow, literally!" Seemingly out of nowhere, a voice said, "Oh, he'll eventually make it." Sara jumped up and turned to look behind her. There was a man standing there, probably thirty years old or so. He apologized saying, "I'm sorry, I shouldn't have scared you like that. Please sit back down, I'll leave." Sara shook her head slightly as if to clear her mind. "Oh, no it's ok. I just didn't know anyone else was around." The man nodded his head towards Robert's grave, "Someone you knew?"

Sara turned to look at the grave marker and then said his name out loud. She looked back at the man, but he was walking away. She called to him, "Wait!"

The man stopped and turned back. "Sir, you can sit here if you want." She wasn't one to talk to random strangers, especially in a cemetery, she thought to herself. The man returned and motioned for Sara to sit down first. He sat on the other end of the bench. The man looked at the grave marker saying, "Robert, I take it a friend or someone special?" Without looking at the man, she said in a low tone, "He was my brother." The man smiled, "You mean he *is* your brother. He's just in a different place now." Sara first thought was, *"what an odd thing to say."* She thought for a moment before asking, "You really believe that?"

The man nodded his head, not saying anything at first, but then remarked, "I don't merely believe it, I know it's true. It's just something you know in your heart. It's not a wish or a dream, you just know that person is still who they were to you, just different. I'll bet he wasn't just your brother, but a good friend as well." Sara wondered how this person knew that.

Why would somebody with this message just show up out of nowhere by coincidence.

The man continued, "You know, he's still here for you. No matter what, all the good things, the good memories, they are alive and well. No one can take those things away from you, they can't take him away from you, unless you let them." The man stood. Sara looked up at him and opened her mouth to say something but wasn't sure what. He smiled and continued, "Sara, I'm sure your brother is really proud of you, and he misses you as much as you miss him." Sara just nodded and looked back at Robert's grave.

She heard the man's footsteps as he walked away. She turned after a bit to see him walk past a large monument and out of sight on the other side. Her eyes widened as the realization struck her that this man had said her name. He had called her Sara, but she hadn't told him her name. She jumped up and ran towards the monument that the man had walked around, but she didn't see him anymore. She looked from one side to the other, but he was gone. She looked behind her towards Robert's grave, but still saw no one.

She walked slowly back and sat down on the bench. She thought about what Jill had said the day before. *'I like to think in some ways, sometimes they might speak through other people.'* Was this what Jill was talking about, Sara wondered. She looked back again, just to make sure the man or no one else was there. She turned to face Robert's grave and said out loud, "So, was that weird or what?" After the encounter with the stranger, she half- expected Robert to answer her in an audible voice. She smiled as she began talking conversationally to her brother, "Hey! I met this lady, Jill. I think you would like her. I'm supposed to be helping her write her life story. I sure wish you were here to help me."

She turned and looked around the cemetery again to see if the man was still there but saw no one. She thought about what the man had said just a few minutes earlier, *'You know he's still here for you.'* She turned back to look at Roberts grave marker and asked, "Are you really? Are you here? So anyway, this lady Jill, she's just started telling me her story. She was in a German concentration camp during WWII when she was just a kid. I'm not sure how I'm supposed to be helping her, but it's part of my court thing.

"I guess I haven't told you about that. It's not my proudest moment.

"My god Robert, I miss you so much. If we could go back and do things over, I would do anything, anything Robert, so you would be here with me right now." The tears began anew. Sara hadn't wept like that while thinking of Robert in quite some time. Her grief felt different this time though. It wasn't a time of anguish. It was simply a time of tears expressing the love she still had in her heart for her brother. She composed herself and stood. She walked over to the grave marker, put her hand to her mouth and kissed the tips of her fingers. She slowly placed her fingers on the top of the marker and held them there. As her tears flowed down both cheeks, she said to her brother, "I miss you, big guy." She wiped away the tears as she walked away and then laughed out loud as she imagined Robert calling after her saying, "Love you too, Dork."

Chapter 13:

As Sara sat down the following Saturday at Jill's, she noticed that Jill did not seem her upbeat self. Sara asked her if she was feeling alright. Jill responded, "Oh yes, I'm fine, my dear. Thank you for asking." Sara commented, "You seem different, is something wrong?" Jill smiled, sighed heavily saying, "Lots of thoughts running through my head is all. I figured it's time to start telling you the hardest part of my story. I have for the most part refrained from dredging up most of those memories throughout my life. I shared only a couple of brief things in a family album that my nieces put together some years back. This week, I've been going over the memories I have of that very difficult time, and I guess that shows. I'm sorry, I didn't think it showed that easily on my face." She smiled, reached across the table and patted Sara's hand saying, "It's alright, it's part of the process. Why don't you tell me about your week first?"

Sara shrugged her shoulders, "Well, it wasn't very exciting really. I visited Robert's grave, which I try to do every week. It helps me, you know, comforts me when I talk to him."

Sara looked down at the table. "I miss him so much. I'm doing better I think, but I feel like I'm going on with my life, and that makes me feel guilty. Part of me feels like that's not fair to Robert." Jill smiled as she shared her thoughts. "Obviously I never met Robert, but from the way you describe him and the relationship the two of you had, it's hard for me to imagine that he would not want you to go on with your life. That doesn't mean you would forget about him. You'll always have the memories of the good times with him and all your conversations and life events. Don't get me wrong, your memories of the difficult times of the last year or so won't ever go away. I know that firsthand, and what we are doing here is a testament to that. I don't want to sound too bold as though I knew him, but I think he would probably tell you right now that the best thing you could do to honor his memory is to do exactly that - go on with your life.

"I think he would still want you to make him proud, but you can't do that if you stay stuck where you've been." Sara finally raised her head and looked at Jill. She gave Jill a half-hearted smile and affirmed, "I know you're right. It's just so hard."

Sara paused a moment and then with a quiver in her voice she continued, "It just hurts so much still."

She fought to gain her composure and keep her wits about her so she wouldn't completely break down in tears. Sara realized again that it had been quite a while since she had done exactly that, sobbed uncontrollably like she had for so many months the previous year. She took a deep breath, determined to hold back her tears. "I think I'm going to be ok, and I couldn't have said that six months ago probably."

It was Jill's turn now to take a deep breath, and began, "Ok, during the time I've spent with you, I have actually had more recollections of those early years. Like I said previously, we had it much better off than many in Guernsey. For me, being only six, and being spared many of the hardships I later learned about others, I do realize how fortunate I was. This was probably one of those times when it was better to stay unaware of everything that was happening around me.

We've talked about how the Germans wanted everything to seem as if nothing had changed. I still attended school, and it was more or less, life as usual for a time.

"It wasn't too long though, and everyday things to started being in short supply. Most basic stuff we take for granted almost became luxuries. Things as simple as coffee and tea. Fresh meat became scarce within six months. Remember how last time we talked about how difficult times can bring out the worst in people? It also makes people compromise. I guess what I mean by that is that people will do things they wouldn't ordinarily do, just to survive or provide for their family.

"I suppose in many ways it's justified. That's the way most everybody looked at the black market which became almost a lifeline for those that found their way into it or made connections. Store owners had their secret stashes of different items and would sell those things at a premium to those who had the cash to pay for them. As I believe I said before, I never knew for sure if my parents' bought things through that black market, but they almost assuredly did. Of course, like others, it would have been to feed our family.

"Another thing that being so young protected me from was knowing about or being exposed to a lot of the brutality. It was much later when I learned about some of our fellow islanders being shot.

"I remember hearing some of the other kids at school talking about a neighbor having been dragged out of their home, and they never saw them again. Or I learned about one of their neighbor's teenage sons having been shot while trying to escape the island. There are some excellent books written by people that were older at the time and witnessed firsthand much of what I just described."

At that point, Jill paused and looked away. Sara waited a bit before saying, "I think I know what you mean about it being kind of a blessing that you were pretty young during that time. One of the first days we talked… Wait!" Sara thumbed back through her notebook stopping at a page towards the front and exclaimed, "Here it is!" Sara read the words she had written that first day she met Jill. "I have often used the phrase that I was old enough to remember, but young enough not to care. In many ways it was a blessing that I was only six years old when the Germans came to the island." Sara bit her lower lip, and her voice broke a little as she looked off to the side before saying, "It might be easier if I had been only 6 years old with all the things that happened to me the last couple of years."

Sara wasn't sure why that particular thought came to her mind right then, but she thought back to a time when she was running through the house and just when she was about to open the front door, Robert opened it to come in and smacked her right in the head. She gave a slight laugh under her breath, thinking how weird it was for that memory to be the one that popped into her head at this moment. Sara shook her head slightly as if to clear her mind and then looked back at Jill.

Jill once again reached across the table and put her hand on Sara's, "I think you really do understand Sara, I appreciate that." Jill took a deep breath before continuing. "Well, now we get to where things get even worse. It had been two full years already since the Germans first took over Guernsey and the other islands. I was 8 years old now. I learned the details much later about why what happened next did so. The U.S. had entered the war almost one year before in December of 1941. There was fighting all over Europe and even into Africa. At one point, the Allies had taken about 200 German prisoners in Persia. Today Persia is known as Iran. It was thought that they were merely German citizens, and not soldiers fighting against Great Britain or the other allied countries.

"That infuriated Hitler, and he gave an order that for every German citizen detained, he wanted 10 British citizens sent to camps in Germany. The only place they knew that had that many British citizens under German control was on the islands they occupied. That is the first time I recall it seeming like people were starting to panic.

"I remember Mother rushing into the house, calling for my father. She had a newspaper folded in her hand and she held it up to my father, pointing frantically at something on the front page. My father grabbed the newspaper and stood there with his mouth hanging slightly open. Then he slammed the newspaper down on the table almost knocking over a small vase that was sitting there. It was obvious he was angry, but I couldn't hear most of their conversation. I did hear my mother say, "What are we going to do?" Then Father shook his head and left the house in a hurry. What was on the front page of that paper my mother had brought in the house was the official order, informing the residents of Guernsey of the deportations that were to take place. I think my mother and father didn't truly believe they we would be deported, but I could tell they were still very nervous.

"There had begun hushed conversations in the other room where I purposely couldn't hear gave me a clue that something different was happening. Even the look on people's faces in town had changed.

"My mother never included me in their discussions or plans. That's one reason I have felt as though many times I was just along for the ride. I didn't really know what was going on. The day my mother brought that newspaper home and then my father stormed out of the house, I went to the table where my father had slammed down the newspaper. I didn't really read it, but remember the words, "British subjects", and also the words, "transferred to Germany". Again, I didn't understand what that meant.

"I found out much later that Hitler had issued the deportation order months before, but because of the wording, those in charge on the island didn't follow through with his order. Apparently, there was no specific time frame set forth in the order for the deportations to begin. Hitler most likely assumed any order he gave was followed immediately. Ironically it was the Swiss who inadvertently alerted Hitler that his orders had not been carried out.

"In their attempts to negotiate an exchange of injured soldiers and civilians it made Hitler aware that his order to round up thousands of British subjects had never been carried out. "Hitler sent a new order demanding the deportations be carried out at once. That is why everything moved so fast at that point.

"It was the middle of September when the order came from Hitler and was posted in the newspaper. It was only a few weeks from my 8th birthday. I had no idea at the time that before I turned eight, I would no longer be living on the island of Guernsey, the only place I had ever called home. The real horrors of that awful time were just beginning. Let's give it a rest for now. I need to really think about everything I want or ought to say beyond this point. Bringing back these memories is hard, but I know if my story is going to be told, then I need to go through it. I hope you understand, my dear?"

Sara's face registered disappointment as she thought, "Man! Just when we were getting to the serious stuff." She understood, though. She was very familiar with the struggle of not wanting to remember certain things. Jill playfully slapped her hands down on the table.

She stood, signaling the visit as over. Sara gathered her things, tucked her notebook in her backpack and thanked Jill.

When they got to the front door, Sara turned and looked at Jill. She started to say something but then stopped, trying to find the words. For the first time, Sara reached out and hugged Jill, telling her, "I hope you have a good week." Jill held back a tear as she responded, "You too, Sara."

Notice in the Jersey and Guernsey newspaper
announcing deportation orders

Guernsey citizens lined up hoping to get some meat and
other goods during occupation. Many of these citizens
would be on these same streets as they were lined up
and marched to waiting ships to be deported to
Germany.

Chapter 14:

The following Saturday as Jill met her at the front door, Sara could tell there was more of a seriousness in Jill's demeanor. Jill was smiling though and greeted her with, "Hello Sara, how was your week?" "Pretty normal I guess," said Sara. Jill motioned towards the table saying, "I think we should get right down to business today, if that's ok." Sara sat down and took out her notebook and pen.

Sara looked across the table and saw that Jill was staring off to the side, not looking across the table at her. Sara still sensed something was wrong, so she wanted to make sure Jill was okay with continuing as planned. She was about to say something when Jill must have sensed it and turned finally to face Sara and held her hand up.

"Sara, I'm alright, really. I could see the concerned look when you first arrived. I so appreciate that you noticed or thought something might be amiss. It's nothing really, but as we move forward now, there might be sometimes I need to stop and gather my thoughts and especially my emotions. But, if we are going to do this, let's do it.

"Let's make it count and do the story justice. How does that sound?" Sara smiled and gave her two thumbs up. Jill noticed Sara's smile become even wider and asked, "What is it?" "When I gave you the two thumbs up, that's...that's what Robert always would do to tell me everything was okay, or that I did a good job. That's cool though, like you said before, it's those memories that I can really hold on to and not just feel sad that he's gone. Okay Jill, you're in charge. I've been looking forward to hearing what happened next."

Jill began. "To summarize a little, it had been two years now since the Germans took over Guernsey. Most food items were starting to get scarce. Those who could get things through the black market were finding it difficult even if they had the money to buy things. Things definitely went from bad to worse and, I have thought about those who remained on the island still had three more years to suffer through. Not only three more years of occupation, but three more years of little to no food, and medicines that had become extremely difficult to find. The biggest difference, though, was that for those who stayed on the island and were not sent to Germany, they at least had a certain amount of freedom that we did not have.

"It was early morning, Sept. 15, 1942, when there was a pounding on our front door. I am sure my mother and father knew what that meant. I stood back in the doorway that led to the front room. When my father opened the door, there was a German officer standing there with two soldiers holding rifles. The officer handed my father a piece of paper and gruffly stated, "By order of der Führer, you will report immediately to the Gaumont Theatre where you will be given further instructions for deportation. Keep your personal items to one garment bag. You have one hour to report."

"The officer made an about-face and stiffly walked away, along with the two soldiers that had been by his side. My father called after the officer, demanding to speak to someone else. The officer ignored him, and then was gone.

"I could see the anguish sweep across my mother's face. I asked her what was wrong, what was happening. Mother put her hands on my shoulders and looked at me sternly, "Listen to me - go get dressed, dress warm and get your big coat. In fact, put on two of everything and don't ask any more questions." I did as I was told, still not really understanding what was happening.

"I had heard the officer mention "deportation" but didn't really understand what that meant. The only thing I remembered was that he said we had to go to the Gaumont Theatre. I dressed and went back into the front room. My mother and father were scurrying around the apartment, grabbing things and putting them in a suitcase. I remember sitting by the front window and looking down toward the street. Everyone on the street looked like they were in a hurry. I saw mothers practically dragging their children down the walkways, and people carrying bags, boxes and personal items, knocking frantically on others' doors. As I read the history later, I understood they were most likely leaving valuables with friends or relatives that perhaps were not being deported. People were running to the bank as well.

"One of the things my father grabbed before leaving for the theatre was the bag with his dental tools. He wasn't sure they would allow him to take them, but as it turned out, that decision might have literally saved my life. I'll save that part for later." Jill saw that Sara had been writing frantically and asked, "Do you need to take a break?" Sara shook her head, "No, please keep going, unless you need to stop for a bit."

Jill smiled, saying, "Well let's pause for a bit then and I will show you a couple of photos that might help paint a better picture of what was going on that dreadful day."

Jill took a couple of pictures out from a box that lay on the table. She laid one in front of Sara. "This is a picture of the Gaumont Theatre where we had to go to be registered for the deportation. Being I was two years older now, and I think this was the first time I sensed some fear. To see the anguish and worry on everyone's faces, even if I didn't understand everything that was happening…it made it real. This picture you see was taken of the theatre in Guernsey. It was during the time when a German movie was being shown for Hitler's birthday celebration. Ever since the occupation began, there were German flags and swastikas all over town."

Sara pointed at a face towards the top of the picture and said, "That's Hitler, right?" Jill nodded and replied with a firm, "Yes!" The next picture Sara saw was a group of people with some sitting and some standing. She started to ask about it as Jill commented, "I'm not sure where this picture was taken but it was on one of the islands when people were ordered to go await deportation.

"This may not have been on Guernsey, but a visual sometimes paints a better picture, so to speak, and that's why I have it."

Gaumont Theatre, where British citizens were ordered to
gather to prepare for deportation.

German soldiers marching through streets of the Channel
Islands. Any sound, similar to the snap of their boots sends
chills through Jill still to this day.

Chapter 15:

Jill continued, "I remember it was unusually cold that day. I guess that added to the gloom people were feeling. Again, I didn't understand everything that was happening. Mother had simply said we had to take a trip. My memories of trips to that point were outings on the family boat, and picnics in the countryside, or trips to the beach...happy times.

"Even at eight years old though, I could see the confused and worried looks on people's faces. We were made to line up, names were called, and identifications checked. We waited a long time, but then after all that we were told to go home. That actually happened several times to a lot of the people who were eventually deported. I imagine whoever was in charge wasn't communicating with the person at the other end of wherever they were going to be taking people. In any event, the last time we reported to the theatre was about ten days later I think, on September 26.

"We learned later that a ship had already taken a group from Jersey a day or so earlier. Sark was the smallest of the islands, and only nine people were taken from there along with the Jersey group."

Jill slowly put her hand to her mouth and closed her eyes. Sara sat waiting to hear what she was going to say next, thinking it must be something serious. Jill raised her head, and she gazed above Sara as she quietly shared, "Sadly, two people on Sark committed suicide rather than submit to an unknown fate." She lowered her head to look back at Sara as she continued. "Another group from Guernsey left on boats two days later. In total, there were 825 of us deported from Guernsey. The total from all the islands was a little over 2000.

"Once again, we were summoned to the Gaumont Theatre. We had to line up, and another roll call was taken. Gradually, groups were led away by soldiers carrying rifles. People had lined the streets in support as we walked the five or six blocks to the harbor people waved, blew kisses, and I saw some simply with their heads bowed, praying. I don't remember anyone specific that day. Some of the people who had gathered to bid us all farewell were crying, but no one had smiles on their faces." Sara interrupted her to ask, "Couldn't people just decide not to show up to be boarded on the boats or whatever?" Jill shook her head as she answered, "Oh no my dear."

"One of the first things the Germans did when they took over the island was to make everyone register. They had to register their address and names of everyone in their family. That way they controlled everyone. Because of that, they knew if someone didn't show up. If they found you later, you would most likely be sent to jail and then deported anyway. Maybe even treated more harshly and then possibly sent to a worse place. So pretty much everyone complied out of fear.

"When we arrived at Saint Peter Port, the wind was blowing off the sea, making the atmosphere even more dismal. I remember looking back towards the town and hearing patriotic songs being sung by those who had gathered to watch. Even though they had done so just an hour before, they lined us up and took roll again. That is one thing I remember vividly throughout the entire ordeal that started that September day, the constant roll calls. I suppose they were verifying that everyone that was supposed to be there, was, and nobody had run off or disappeared. I guess there were some who tried to hide or escape, but I never really heard or read anything about that for sure. One by one a German in uniform would go down the line, call names and check identification papers.

"We were lined up on the pier, and up ahead I could see people walking onto a large fishing boat. We had been told we were being taken to San Marlo in France, but that was all. Of course, no one knew where we were going beyond that, and anyone who asked questions was ignored. As we made our way onto the boat, I was overwhelmed by the horrible smell of fish and that acrid smell of oil, grease, and gas or diesel fuel. Those odors have stayed with me to this day.

"We were all forced to go down into the hull of the ship. It was dark and damp and smelled really bad. Mother and Father pushed us all to the front section, and my brother and I huddled together in one corner. I heeded my mother's constant scolding, and I didn't ask any more questions, I just sat there. We sat for what seemed like hours, but I really don't know how long it was. As we heard the engines start up and felt the ship begin to move, I heard ladies starting to cry. Some of the people I could hear praying out loud, but it was too dark to really see much.

"My brother snuggled against me, and from what little light there was, I could see my mother and father just staring down at the floor.

"I think maybe I've said before, I never had a close relationship with my father or even my mother for that matter. Father was always a positive person and at least acted like adversity didn't bother him. At that moment, though, he looked completely defeated. When I tried to ask a question, he would look sternly at me, and always said the same thing, which was, "Say nothing." I grew to hate that phrase, but I knew he meant exactly what those two words said, and I would remain silent after that.

"I was used to being on a boat, so the motion on the waves didn't bother me or the rest of our family. It had been very windy when we boarded the boat. That made the sea extremely rough. It wasn't long before people started getting sick. That is something that still sticks with me to this day, the sounds and eventually the smell from people throwing up. The boat was rising and falling constantly on the waves. I remember hearing the creaking of the wood on the boat. Up and down, and sometimes hitting a wave that would rock us back and forth. It made it hard to stay in one place.

"There were no toilets and there were too many people crammed into the small space.

"So, there was no place for people that were getting sick. A lot of people were getting seasick, and the stench became unbearable. My brother and I huddled closer together and I pulled my coat up over my nose to try and get away from the constant smell of vomit. I was confused, and for the first time, I personally felt scared about everything that was happening. As I have said, my young age had protected me from a lot of the fear and anxiety that others older than me had been feeling up to that point. That was the first time I remember crying about what was taking place. I just sat there with my face buried in my coat, hugging my brother.

"It seemed like forever, but we finally heard the engines power down and we could hear shouting up on the deck. After the ship stopped, a German soldier appeared in the doorway and yelled in German, 'Alle raus, Alle raus!', Get out, Get out!

"When we came out onto the deck, it was dark, and the wind made it extra cold. Some people were still getting sick as we were led down the gangway and off the ship. Several soldiers with guns forced us all into a line as they directed us down the pier. We reached a roadway in front of a dark building and stopped.

"We were made to line up a few rows deep. Once more, another roll call was taken. I just remember it being very cold and we were hungry. I wasn't even sure when had been the last time I had eaten.

"Several people came up to where we were lined up, and I'm not sure if they were soldiers or what, but they started passing out pieces of bread and a sausage to everyone. My mother broke off pieces and handed them to my brother and me. The bread was stale, and the sausage didn't have much flavor, but we still ate it. We weren't sure when we would have our next meal.

"After the roll call was completed, we stood around, out in the cold, and waited for a long time late into the night. Suddenly several soldiers started yelling orders towards all of us and motioning with their rifles for us to move. They led us further down the road and around a couple of buildings, eventually leading us to the train tracks. None of the soldiers were speaking English, and I didn't know what they were saying. They weren't violent, but they were pushing and shoving everyone along as we were boarded onto train cars. We at least had seats now, and it was a little warmer being out of the wind, standing on the street.

"I remember later reading about how the Jews were treated, all crammed shoulder-to-shoulder into box cars like cattle for days on their way to the camps, with no food or water. We had no idea where we were being taken next. It was a long time before the train finally started to move. I just remember sitting and feeling bored and hungry still. The train eventually started moving and while it was still dark out.

"It wasn't until sometime the following day that two German soldiers came on board and passed out more bread and sausage. The train traveled all that day and through the night. On the second day, once again soldiers came through the train car and this time handed out some grapes and apples. That is all we had for three days. The train would stop at several towns along the way. Each time it stopped, people became antsy, wondering what was next, and whether this was where we were getting off. During the day, I was able to look out the window.

"The countryside was beautiful for the most part, but the trip dragged on and on and I thought it would never end.

"There was no heat on the train, and even though there were seats, it was crowded. After three days, the train finally stopped for the last time. We were in a place called Dorsten. I heard someone on the train say at that point, we were indeed in Germany now. This time, soldiers came on the train and ordered everyone to get off.

"They lined us up again and roll call was taken. At that point, they separated the men from the women and children. I asked my mother where they were taking my father, but she ignored me. We were all hurried onto buses. Myself, my brother, and my mother went on one bus, while my father got taken to another bus with all the men. This was the first time we had been separated.

"As the bus began down the road I looked outside as we passed by several buildings. There were some buildings that had fallen, maybe from bombing. I could see a canal. I couldn't really see that there was an actual town. The bus eventually passed through a large wire gate into an area with a bunch of buildings, built in even rows. The buildings were pretty run down. The place looked desolate and abandoned. There were long buildings in the center.

"The whole place was surrounded by tall wire fencing with rolls of barbed wire along the top. There were several tall wooden structures that reminded me of a tree house. I later found out those tall things were guard towers.

"I later learned that Dorsten had been a Polish POW camp. It had been left in a state of disrepair and what I can best describe as complete filth. I guess nothing had been done to the place since they moved all the POWs someplace else. We were lined up and counted. I don't remember a lot about being at Dorsten, other than it was probably one of the most depressing places I have ever spent time at.

"I'm sure a lot of the adults were thinking that this is where they brought us all to die. We ended up being there for about six very long weeks. They kept the men separated, but they allowed men to visit with their wives and families during that time. I remember seeing my father from time to time.

"Sadly, three people that arrived there with us from Guernsey and Jersey died before we left Dorsten. One was a child only four months old. I think they were buried there near the camp.

"I know after the war some of those who had died and been buried in various places were eventually returned to their hometown and given a proper burial. Some though, no one knew where they were buried."

Jill paused, took a deep breath, before saying, "OK, I think that's enough. I hope I didn't bore you to death?" Sara exclaimed, "Are you kidding? Of course not!"

Sara was disappointed that Jill had stopped, but she also knew sharing this part of her story was very emotional for Jill. It was definitely emotional for Sara listening. She couldn't imagine how this young, eight-year-old girl came through it all and go on to become this elegant lady sitting across the table from her. As Sara walked out the door, she turned and, in a pleading, tone asked, "Jill, I don't have school tomorrow, so would it be alright if I came over so we could continue? I mean, you know, if you're not busy." Jill smiled saying in response, "I think that's a wonderful idea. We might as well keep the wheels turning now that they have started rolling. I will see you tomorrow at the same time if that works for you." Sara gleefully answered, "Okay, see you tomorrow."

She started to leave but turned back and gave Jill a spontaneous hug like the last time, then hurried down the steps.

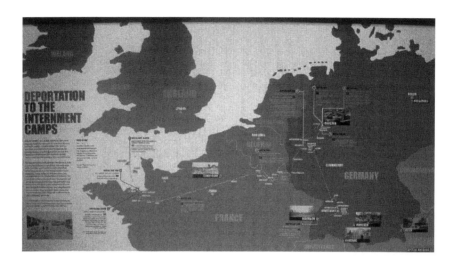

Map showing ship and train routes to the German
internment camps

The internment camp at Dorsten known as Stalag VI-J

Three Channel Islanders died during the six weeks in
the horrible conditions at the Dorsten camp.

Chapter 16:

Sara sat across the table from Jill the next day, pen and notebook in hand. Jill smiled and remarked, "Well, I can see you are ready to get started, so, let's do it. Tell me what you have in your notes where we left off." Sara flipped one page back and answered, "You had finished up yesterday saying that three people died during the time you were at the camp there in Dorsten. Did they die from disease, or what?" Jill shook her head before responding, "I'm not really sure. The conditions were so poor It's surprising there weren't more that got sick and died. The sheer fact of living in that place with very little food. There was no clean water either, but I imagine it was just sickness. It could have been heart problems or something like that. Lord knows, if you could die from a broken heart, it will happen at Dorsten. The baby that died, I really don't know how or why."

"After another, what had become the routine roll call, we were led into these long buildings. I guess you would call them dorms. The buildings were old and smelled of mildew and sewage. The only light was coming from the doorway.

"Some windows were so dirty that light could barely get through. Lined up along the walls were bunk beds made of wood. The beds had thin layers of straw covered with a blanket as a mattress. No one seemed sure what to do but eventually women started moving to the different beds, claiming their spots. My brother and I followed mother and she lifted my brother up onto a top bunk as I climbed up from the end. I looked down as my mother sat down on the bottom bunk and just hung her head.

"The sewage smell was pervasive because there was almost no sanitation to speak of. Everyone started claiming a bunk. Most of the children had to share a bunk along with their mother. I remember telling my mother that I needed to go to the bathroom but there was no bathroom really. At some point we were shown what it was we had to do for a bathroom. First of all, there was very little privacy. Our toilet consisted of a bucket, just a metal bucket. After doing what we had to do in the bucket, we then had to pour it into a crevice in the concrete floor where I guess it eventually drained into the ground somewhere. Our dorm had a constant smell of urine and human waste.

"No one had bathed since we left Guernsey, so that added to the awful odors around the room.

"I am sure a lot of people there wondered how long they could really take living in these conditions. Ultimately, we ended up spending about six weeks in the Dorsten camp. I remember one of the ladies saying that she expected we would be back home by Christmas. As I said, we only spent about six weeks there in Dorsten, but I doubt anyone there imagined it would ultimately be three Christmas's before we would ever see our homes again.

"My brother and I sat on the hard bunk and just looked around the room. The looks on everyone's faces told a bleak story. It was hard to imagine our lives having any kind of a happy ending. A couple of soldiers came into the dormitory with bags and started passing out bread and sausages to us all. The bread was hard, and the sausage was greasy, and it had a lot of fat. We ate it, though. We were starving. We wouldn't get anything different to eat until the following day.

"We weren't allowed outside until the next day. The next morning, I walked outside. I got a few steps from the door and just looked back and forth.

When I saw the area inside the camp, I noticed that it had no trees or plants of any kind. It was just dirt and mud. There really was nothing to do out there.

"We still welcomed the opportunities to go outside where we could at least get away from the smell from inside the dorm buildings. I think it was that next day that we saw my father again. When I saw my father, I hugged him, but he remained stiff. as though he didn't notice me. He talked to my mother about where they had placed all the men. It was a similar building. Apparently, separating the men was to give the women and children somewhat more privacy. I don't know that the Germans really cared what we thought or how we felt, though.

"I wouldn't describe any of the time we spent in the German camps as pleasant or ideal, but those six weeks in Dorsten seemed forever, and were the worst of all. This is partly because no one knew what was coming next. We had been told that the Dorsten camp was temporary. What made things worse was there was never any kind of routine, nor was there a sense of community. Everyone seemed to just remain in a depressed mood all day long.

"Since there was nothing to do, I guess it was depression combined with boredom. At Dorsten we were allowed outside, but it was such a dismal place. The whole area I later learned was just a big industrial area near the canal. The same canal I had seen from the bus on our way from the train. The area had been bombed quite a bit, so there wasn't much we could see that was going on outside the camp itself. The next place became our permanent home for the remainder of the war, and there is a lot to that story I'll get to shortly.

"As bad as it was for us at Dorsten, I can't even imagine what the Polish prisoners went through living there. The days dragged on there with nothing to do. As best I can remember, for the most part we only got one meal a day - that is, if you could call what they gave us a meal. Other than the constant stale bread and occasional sausage, about the only other thing we had was a watery soup. I'll tell you more about that soup later.

"After six weeks had gone by, a German official of some sort came into the dorm one day and told everyone to gather their belongings because we were leaving. It was November 12.

"I don't think anybody was excited by the announcement. I am sure some thought, they couldn't be taking us some place worse, but no one talked about that. I guess everyone didn't want to imagine that something really could be worse. It would have been scary to think exactly what "worse" might be like.

"We gathered what few clothes and other things we had and walked outside. After roll call, we were led to buses and trucks again where they loaded us. Then they drove through the same gate we had come through six weeks before, and then out of the camp. I looked out the window and wrinkled my nose as I looked back at the stark landscape and drab buildings where we had spent the last six weeks. I think I might have felt a little hopeful at that moment. Some of the ladies remarked that maybe they were finally taking us home. Nothing could have been further from the truth.

"The buses and trucks made their way back to the same train stop where we had arrived six weeks earlier. Soldiers as usual yelled for everyone to get off and line up. By now you can guess what came next, another roll call. After ID's were checked, we boarded the train. This train seemed more crowded than the one before.

"As everyone crowded onto the train, I looked around for my father, but soon realized that everyone on the train car with us were either women or children because they had separated the men again.

"We at least hoped the men were all on other train cars and going with us, wherever that might be. Because it was so crowded, and my brother and I were small enough, we climbed into the luggage racks over the seats with Mother's help. It was nice to be out of the crowd, so to speak. I looked around for a while watching the looks on people's faces. There was murmuring but I really can't remember if I heard anything any of them were saying.

"I had made a couple of friends with kids in Dorsten, and occasionally our eyes would meet, "and we would both just smile. It was another adventure for those of us that still didn't understand everything that was happening around us.

"The train traveled late into the night. There were several stops, and every time we stopped, they made everyone get off, line up, take roll call and then get herded back on the trains. One thing about the British, they are almost always courteous to each.

"That is even whether they know you or not. So, there were never any arguments or fights when we got back on the train after a stop, over who was sitting where, and no accusations of someone taking their seat.

"My brother and I would climb back up into the luggage rack and try to sleep. The train kept going all night, and eventually it became light, but we continued on that interminable journey. In all, we traveled about thirty-six hours. Only once during that trip did anyone come aboard the train car and pass out something resembling food. A large pail of water was put at the front of the train car where everyone could dip a cup into for a drink.

"No one could tell which direction we were going, so there was no way of knowing where they were taking us. Laying down in the luggage racks, I couldn't see much out of the windows of the train car, and no one commented that they recognized anything as the train passed. Sometime in late morning the train came to a final stop. They made us wait for quite a while on the train. My brother and I had climbed down from the luggage rack above, and my brother sat on our mother's lap while I stood on the floor beside them.

"Eventually, a German officer in a much nicer uniform than most of the soldiers came on the train and gave us some instructions. It was obvious he wanted us to know he was in control, but he was not mean. He talked and didn't shout his instructions. We were told to get off the train in an orderly fashion.

"Apparently, several trains had already brought different people from the Channel Islands to this place. It was another camp of some sort, but it looked much cleaner and better kept than where we had just come from. Those who were already settled in the camp were standing in front of the buildings off in the distance just watching the train as we all got off and lined up.

"I found out later that the camp was called Biberach, after the town where it was located. As I looked around and noticed the buildings were similar to the ones in Dorsten, but they were mostly concrete.

"We were led through the gate, and into the camp. There was a building towards the middle that was more than one story tall, but the rest were mostly the long dormitory-type buildings like we had in Dorsten. Beyond the barbed wire fencing I could see different buildings.

"I assumed those buildings were part of a town this place was close to. I looked off in the distance and could see a river. I later learned it was called the Riss, and we were south of the infamous Black Forest. From certain areas of the camp, you could even see the Swiss Alps. At least the surrounding area wasn't as bleak as Dorsten.

"As we lined up for the roll call, I remember it was bitterly cold. The wind was blowing and there was snow everywhere. The wind was that cutting chill that comes over you if you have ever been in that kind of weather. My mother must have looked down and saw me shivering. I remember she wrapped a blanket of wool or horsehair around me. She pinned it in the front with a large metal safety pin, and the thing that stands out the most about that moment is I can still remember how icy cold that big safety pin felt on my chest. One thing everyone knew for sure was that with it being only the middle of November, Winter hadn't even arrived yet and the weather was probably going to get much worse.

"I imagine that most of the adults had concluded we probably would not be home by Christmas. The next question they probably asked themselves was how long we would really be here.

"After a general roll call, we were lined up in more of a single file line and then we had to walk up to a table where German officers were sitting. They were taking everyone's information to register us in the camp. We were led away in groups and taken to different dorm buildings. Each room had 16 bunks, but there were a lot more than 16 people to a room. As we claimed our space, my brother and I climbed up onto one of the bunks. Just like the last place, the mattresses were made of straw and covered with a thin layer of sackcloth or burlap. I remember it wouldn't take long for the straw to became flattened down and we would have to open the cloth covering to try and fluff up the straw. We had fun bouncing on the new, fluffier mattress until mother scolded us for making it flat again.

"We had only been given a couple of things to eat during the thirty-six-hour train ride and I was starving. It wasn't the last time I would be really hungry." Jill took in a deep breath before saying, "I think it's time to take a break. We'll continue next Saturday if that's ok."

Jill stood and stretched as Sara gathered up her notebook, pen, and backpack. As Sara was leaving, Jill remarked, "I'm going to fix us lunch on Saturday.

"So, come around eleven o'clock if that works for you."
Sara gave Jill a hug like she had the last couple of times.
Sara had driven herself the last few times and she
waved to Jill as she drove off.

A women and children's barracks at the Biberach.

Aerial view of the Biberach camp and the town a short distance away

Dormitories at Biberach

Drawing of one of the dorms made by an internee at Biberach

Chapter 17:

Sara walked into Jill's home the following Saturday, excited to continue hearing her story. Jill greeted her with a smile and walked with her to the dining table. Jill held her hand towards one of the chairs, "Have a seat, dear and I'll get our lunch." Sara sat down and waited. A short time later, Jill walked in with a tray and sat it on the table. She put a bowl in front of Sara and a small plate with some bread. Sara looked down at the bowl filled with some type of liquid, -that she assumed was soup. Jill sat down with her own bowl and plate. She said to Sara, "I thought it might give you a different perspective to experience what one of our typical, and few meals were like in the German camps. This is Swede soup. Here in the U.S., swede is a type of turnip."

Sara picked up the piece of bread that was almost completely hard. She looked back down at the bowl and scrunched up her nose. Jill smiled and wished her, "Bon Appetit." Jill watched as Sara picked up her spoon and dipped it in the bowl, stirring it around. She took up a spoonful with some small bits of what she figured was swede or turnip in a very watery liquid. She took a sip and swallowed hard.

She swirled her tongue around in her mouth to get the taste washed out as best she could. The turnip was slightly bitter-tasting and the liquid nearly tasteless. She picked up the piece of bread and struggled to pull a bit off with her teeth.

Jill watched as Sara chewed for a long time and finally swallowed. Jill took a coffee mug and poured some brown-looking warm liquid. She handed it to Sara saying, "Here, this will wash down that bread." Sara took a good gulp of the liquid and again her face winced, and she swallowed hard as she struggled to swallow it down. Jill chuckled a little as she commented, "Coffee and tea became almost non-existent early on, and the adults in the camp would make coffee out of crushed and roasted acorns, or other nuts they could find.

Jill smiled, saying, "That's enough my dear, I don't expect you to finish any of this. I actually have a real lunch prepared." She cleared the table and returned with a big glass of lemonade that Sara took big thankful gulps of, washing down the taste of the acrid coffee and bitter soup.

Jill put a platter with several different small sandwiches, grapes, and crackers on the table. She said with a smile, "Does this look better?" Sara laughed as she responded, "Honestly, I was a bit disappointed when you wouldn't let me finish that wonderful dishwater-like soup. It accomplished what you said, because actually tasting it was much different than just having you describe what they fed you, or me reading about it. I can't even imagine the real hunger you experienced at times.

"Other than missing a meal because I was busy, I've never gone hungry. I would assume you ate whatever they gave you whether you liked it or not." Jill nodded, answering, "You get past the taste pretty quick when you have actual hunger pangs. They ate the rest of their lunch in relative silence, and while Sara ate, she thought a lot about what Jill and her family experienced with the food they were given.

Jill finally spoke up and continued with her story. "Once things more or less got established in the camp, we got used to the meager food. We usually got the Swede soup, or soup made with small bits of cabbage, but it rarely had anything else in it.

"If we were lucky, the soup would sometimes have a few small pieces of some type of meat. I remember one time, someone bringing a bag into the dorm and setting it on the table. One of the ladies started taking several loaves of dark-colored bread out of the bag and placed them on the table. My eyes widened a little and then closed as I turned away. I don't remember what any of the ladies said at the time, but I think they were words of disgust. When I looked back, one of the ladies had cut slices from one of the loaves and I could see things moving in the bread. Several ladies shook their heads and simply began picking maggots out of the bread." Sara's mouth dropped open, and she put her hand to her mouth in horror, looking like she might throw up.

Jill reached across the table and took Sara's other hand, saying "I'm sorry, I know some of this is hard to hear, but you wanted the real story." Sara nodded, not looking directly at Jill, then responded as she slowly shook her head back and forth, "No need to apologize Jill. If you're going to tell your story, it has to be real. Otherwise, there's no sense in telling it. It's hard to hear how you and all of the people were treated, and it's really different hearing it firsthand instead of just hearing someone lecture from a history book or essay.

"As hard as it is to hear, it's got to be harder for you to bring up all these memories." Jill truly appreciated the understanding and compassion that Sara was showing. Jill continued, "As bad as we had it, it was years later that I learned how in a lot of ways we were some of the lucky ones.

"I know it might sound absurd to say we were lucky, but to learn how the Jewish people were treated, and learning that many of their camps were basically slave labor camps where people were literally worked to death. Of course, - that's besides the real holocaust that took place with the Jews. There were several Jewish people in the Biberach camp and at some point, they were taken away and we never saw them again. The Germans expected our camp to run smoothly, and they left it to the internees to organize our own form of order, schooling, activities, etc.

"That's where it was really different for us compared to the regular POW camps and the labor camps. Those from the Channel Islands tried as much as possible to make it like our own little town. As we got settled in, there were two teachers that helped organize schooling. Others organized activities.

"It gave us all at least some sense of normalcy and routine." Sara interrupted her as she asked, "How were you able to have school with no books?" Jill responded, "Especially for the younger kids, if you have people that are actually good teachers, a lot of educating can be done without books. Books help, of course, but I look back on it now and realize that in a lot of ways, we got an education that money and books couldn't buy.

"We definitely learned a lot of life lessons and what would be considered social studies. We kept up with the basics like general math and reading and writing. One of the things everyone learned was how to make do with what was available. There were individuals in the camp that were really good artists. Those people especially knew how to use anything available to make a lot of different things.

"After about a month, it was a miracle when the Germans allowed Red Cross packages to start being delivered to the camps. They eventually allowed mail to be sent and received. The letters or telegram- type messages were very few, so it was always exciting to hear something from back home.

"They also started allowing some packages from back home. Packages had always been opened before they arrived, I suppose for security, but you could tell things had been taken. I'm sure many of the Germans didn't have much more than we did, so I guess that was to be expected. We were grateful for anything we got, especially any type of food items.

"As the war dragged on, we would learn later that the people back home, weren't much better off as far as food than we were in the camps. Eventually, the correspondence and the packages stopped." Jill watched as Sara busily took notes. She stopped writing, then looked up at Jill and asked, "What was in the Red Cross packages?" Jill took a picture out from a box and handed it over to Sara. It was a picture of one of the actual Red Cross packages received in the camps.

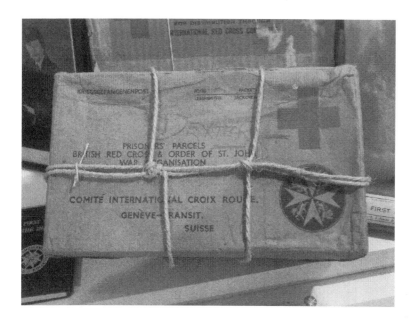

Red Cross package sent to British citizens interned in
the German camps

Jill continued, "For a while we received packages
once a month. I watched as my mother opened the first
package we received and took out the items. There was
tea, a small amount of chocolate, a small can of
condensed milk, and some Players brand cigarettes.

We would cut the figure of a sailor from the cigarette
packs like paper dolls and link them together with
string from the packages. My mother would make that
one can of condensed milk last a whole week.

"She would do it by putting small amounts into a pitcher of water. We had to make everything last as long as we could. We never knew when more items might come, if ever. The adults would take the small amount of tea that was in the packages and reuse it again and again until it didn't even change the color of the water anymore. Remember the coffee made from crushed acorns?"

Sara pressed her lips into a forced smile as she recalled, "Uh, yeah, I can still taste it I think." Jill said, "The men used to make cigarettes out of the grounds after they made the coffee.

"One of the most special items I remember in one of the packages that actually came from a YMCA organization was a children's book called Runaway Home, by Elizabeth Coatsworth." Jill reached into the box sitting to the side of the table and pulled out a well-worn book with a blue hard cover and handed it to Sara, saying "This is the book. A friend sent this to me, and I've kept it all these years." Sara held the book as if it were a precious gem.

She realized she was holding a piece of someone's personal history from WWII.

She opened the book and saw on the inside cover a stamp that said, "War Prisoners Aid, World's Committees YMCA, Geneva Switzerland." On the opposite page was an inscription that read, "Jill Pay, to remind you of your school days at Biberach, 1942." Sara's mouth was slightly open, and she had a look of amazement as Jill continued.

"This was one of only two books that came in the packages, and I read this one so many times I had it memorized word for word." Sara noticed as Jill made the last statement that she had turned her head and was looking out the window, seemingly deep in thought. Sara waited a bit, then asked Jill what she was thinking at that moment. Jill turned back to face her saying, "Whenever I think about this book, I remember how I felt as I read it the first time. The book is about a family, - basically on an adventure moving to a different part of the country. I was happy reading the book, imagining what the kids were experiencing as they traveled, wondering how they felt and imagining their excitement. Then I thought about the freedom that family had and I couldn't relate to that life at all.

"After I read the book the first time, I lay it on the bed and just sat there feeling sad.

"By now I was eight years old, and I was able to comprehend what my reality was. My reality was I lived behind barbed wire, and I really didn't know anything else. I finally got off the bed and walked outside. It had snowed more, and the wind was really cold. I looked across the bare dirt in front of the building we were living in and just stared through the wire fence, and my eyes got watery. I just wanted to go home.

The book Jill had in Biberach, Runaway Home. sent from the YMCA

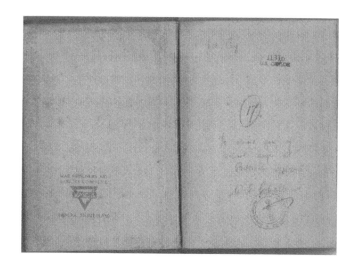

Inside cover of Jill's book, with War Prisoners stamp and inscription

Chapter 18:

"I thought about home a lot at first. We had already lived two years under German occupation back home, so what few things I remembered, I didn't have any sense of what a normal childhood was like, or a normal home life. It was probably good that none of us knew we would be spending more than three years in the camps in Germany. It became the only home I knew for a long time.

"I mentioned earlier about the Red Cross packages and how we made use of everything. People re-used the string and paper that the packages were wrapped in. Sometimes a few clothes would arrive from back home, or through agencies like the Red Cross, but for the most part, we had to make do with the few things we were allowed to carry from home when we were first deported.

"Our shoes wore out over time, and people would use the cardboard from the Red Cross packages to make new soles for shoes." Sara unconsciously looked down at one of her shoes as Jill continued. "We occasionally got paper for drawing and writing. That wasn't very often though.

"People would use the brown paper wrapped around the packages for writing paper and other things like the paper dolls we would make sometimes.

"We had regular classes for school after not too long. I think I did pretty well with my studies. At one point I received an award for high marks. I was so excited. I was called to the front by the teacher. I don't remember what she said, but she handed me a certificate. It was handmade by one of the men in the camp who did drawings and painting." Jill reached again into the box and pulled out a card and handed it to Sara. Sara looked at, exclaiming, "Wow! This is the actual certificate you got?" Jill smiled as she answered, "Yes. I have several things like this that I'll show you in a while. These types of things were really special, and I still cherish them."

Sara held the card and ran her fingers over it lightly as if it was a delicate flower. She turned it over and then back to the front again. She read it aloud, "Biberach 1944 Camp, Junior School Upper Group, Jill Pay British Internee No. 226, Second in term marks, June 29th, 1944".

She marveled at the detail of vines and flowers that bordered the card, and a drawing at the bottom of a camp building. She looked at the date again and remarked, "This was over eighty-five years ago." Jill simply nodded.

Jill continued with her story. "One of the organizations that the Germans thankfully allowed to send things to the camps was a number of YMCA clubs from around the world. Like the one that sent the book I showed you. Some of the items the YMCA sent were musical instruments and clothing. There were some really good musicians that had been deported along with us and they organized a camp orchestra. They even painted on the bass drum their name, Biberach Camp Orchestra." Jill pulled another picture from the box and handed it to Sara. It was a picture of the actual band that ten men and one woman had formed. Jill said, "We always enjoyed when they performed. Anything like that was a distraction from our day-to-day reality. They would put on shows for us as often as they could. Others formed a theatre group and planned plays for the camp. I was never in one of the shows, but I really enjoyed seeing them.

"We had very few school supplies, so we made do with what was available. As I mentioned before, a lot of our art projects were done with scraps from the Red Cross packages. We used the string that came wrapped around the packages, and pieces of burlap type cloth that some items were packed in. I was so thankful for the ladies that organized an actual school for us. I especially liked the art classes and crafts we would make."

Jill walked across the room and opened a drawer in a cabinet that was against the wall. When she returned, she handed a folded piece of paper to Sara. When Sara unfolded it, she saw it was the picture of the tapestry Jill had showed her earlier. She stared at it for a moment before saying, "Wow! So, you really made this?" Jill smiled as she answered, "Yes I did." Sara looked again at the tapestry of flowers made with bright red stitching and other things. "I was probably about 9 or 10 when I made that. It was made from the different scraps that I mentioned." "This is amazing," Sara marveled. I can't believe you still have it after all these years, or I guess you said a relative has it. I would have thought that once all of you were freed, you would have just run out of there as fast as you could."

"Well, we'll get into all that a little later." Jill said. Sara laid the paper on the table and smoothed it out. She kept running her fingers over the areas of the stitching without saying anything more. Finally, Sara remarked in a grateful tone, "Thank you so much for showing me this. It must be really special to still have it after all these years."

Tapestry Jill made while in Biberach

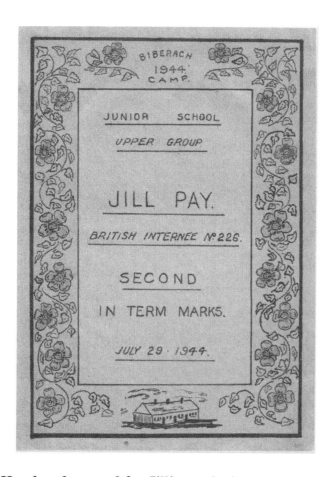

Handmade award for Jill's marks in the school at
Biberach

"I'm really thankful to still have several items
from my time there, considering all the places I've lived
since those years so long ago."

Sara finally pulled her hand away from the tapestry picture. Jill took the paper, folded it, and placed it in the box that had the pictures she had been taking out to show Sara.

Jill said, "Ok, let's get back to it." Jill took on a serious look and said, "My mother spent most of her time with my younger brother and the things she would do with the other ladies. A lot of times I felt like I had been just pushed aside. Thankfully, I had some friends in the camp. One of my best friends was Mary Way. We had known the family back in Guernsey. Mary had a sister named Ann and an older brother named John. I kept in touch with John up until he passed away just a few years ago.

"After four or five months in the camp, it was finally starting to warm up a little as spring was coming. It was towards the end of the month, and a shipment of Red Cross packages was dropped off in the camp.

"Mary and I sat next to each other at the table in our dorm building as the ladies opened their individual packages. My eyes lit up when my mother pulled out a box with a Ball and Jacks game. It was one of the few times I remember my mother smiling in the camp.

"She looked almost happy for the first time in a very long time as she handed me the box. Mary and I ran outside to play. We spent much of our time in the camp playing ball and jacks and playing hopscotch. We would draw hopscotch squares in the dirt and use a flat rock to throw into the squares. There were very few real toys for all of the kids, so we did whatever we could to entertain ourselves.

"At the age Mary and I were, life in the camp became really the only life we knew. We would occasionally talk about things back home, but the previous couple of years weren't the best because of the Germans being in control. We had very few memories of fun things to talk about. We didn't understand that we had missed out on what most would consider a normal childhood. That was another fortunate thing about being young and unaware of how bad things really were. One nice thing in the camp we were living in was after a while there were times, they allowed small groups outside the camp for walks. Mary and I would walk together, and we would watch our parents trade things with local residents.

"They would trade cigarettes and other items they had gotten in the Red Cross packages for fresh vegetables, clothing, and anything else that we didn't have on a regular basis.

"My father being a dentist and having been allowed to bring along some of his dental tools, he was expected to do dental work in the camp and also was taken outside the camp into the town about once a week to provide dental care to townspeople. More on that later.

"One of the special things I have been able to save from all those years ago are the handmade cards like the one I just showed you. One gentleman in particular in the camp was a very talented artist. People would trade things for him to make birthday and Christmas cards. He did some things just for the community as well, like posters advertising the music shows and parades that were organized from time to time. I've seen pictures in books of some of those posters and some of his other drawings. I actually have several cards with his artwork from my time in the camp. I really cherish those things. The happy times or memories of life there were few and far between, but those cards always bring a smile to my face when I look at them."

Jill reached into the box and pulled out a card which she handed to Sara. Her reaction was the same as when she saw the tapestry Jill had made. In fancy cursive script, the card said, "Wishing you a very Happy Birthday." There was a drawing in colored pencil of the barracks- type building that Jill had described before. She could see a guard tower and the camp fencing. On the left side was a drawing of a red, white, and blue ribbon. Jill reached across the table and pointed to the center of the ribbon as she asked, "Do you see the 'V' at the center?" Sara had not really noticed it, but as she looked closer, replied, "Yeah, I guess I see it now." Jill smiled as she remembered and shared, "One of the first acts of rebellion that started early on around Guernsey was people painting a 'V' on signs and buildings.

"The V stood for Victory, meaning the people of Guernsey believed the British would eventually be victorious. It really upset the Germans and there were warnings posted in the local paper that posting a 'V' was against the law. Some people were even put in prison when they were caught painting a 'V' in different places. The same thing continued in the camps.

"The Germans caught on quick and would take away privileges or other things when a 'V' was noticed around the camp. So, people started making them very subtle like the way the artist drew this ribbon. The 'V' looks like it was just part of the tied knot in the middle."

Sara laughed and said, "That's really clever. I can see why this card means so much to you. I can't believe you still have it after all these years." Sara opened the card and read the inscription inside. "FROM MARY MEAD. TO JILL. OCT. 9TH, 1943. WITH BEST WISHES." As she handed the card back, Jill continued,

"We had been in the camp there in Biberach for about a full year by then. It was my second birthday behind the wired fences. It made my birthday special though." Jill reached into the box and pulled out another card which she handed over to Sara. Sara looked at the drawing of a forest with a river running through the middle, and mountains in the background. She read the wording across the top and bottom, "Birthday Greetings"

She opened the card and again read out loud, "Oct. 9, To Jill wishing you a happy birthday, love from Anne 1943."

Sara sat staring at the card, and Jill noticed her eyes getting watery. She reached over and took the card and asked, "Is everything ok?" Sara rubbed at one of her eyes and responded, "I'm ok. I was just thinking about all that you were going through during that whole time. It's pretty amazing that you are sitting here right now talking with me." Jill shook her head, somewhat in disagreement as she said in a compassionate tone, "One thing I know is that I am truly blessed, despite everything I've gone through in life. I think it's pretty amazing Sara, that *you* are sitting here right now talking with *me*." They both laughed softly at that.

Jill pulled another item out of the box and handed it over to Sara. Sara said, "Wow! you have more? These are so awesome." She read the cover, "Greeting" The top half was a drawing of a building with a clock tower that she assumed was part of the camp. She opened the card and read, "To Jill, Wishing her many happy returns of the day. With love from Mummy and Daddy. Biberach, Germany, Oct. 9th, 1943."

Sara just looked at the card for a long time and didn't say anything after she read the words. She finally looked up and saw Jill sitting with her hands folded and looking down at the table. Sara watched for a long, pensive moment. She wondered what thoughts were going through Jill's mind, recalling all of these memories. Finally, Jill looked up saying, "That card actually surprised me, but let's leave it at that."

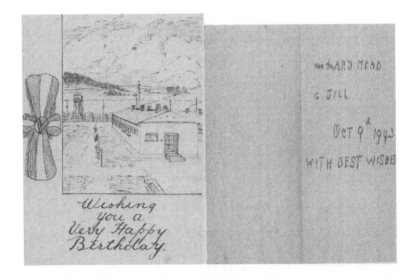

One of Jill's birthday cards from her friend Mary, on the second of three birthdays she spent in Germany

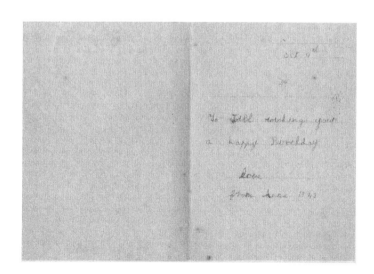

Birthday card from Anne, a friend in the camp

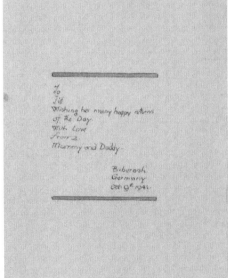

Birthday card from Jill's parents during their time in
Biberach

Chapter 19:

Sara handed the cards back to Jill and watched in silence as Jill returned them to the box. Jill stood, picked up the box, and walked across the room without saying anything. She put the box in a closet and came back to sit down. She reached toward the side of the table and picked up a folder, then opened the folder and pulled out a sheet of paper with some printing on it. Sara saw an official type of seal at the top of the page but wasn't sure what it was. She continued looking at the paper, trying to see what it was when Jill stated, "Well, this is it." "What do you mean?" Sara asked.

Jill picked up a pen and put her signature at the bottom of the paper, then turned it around so it faced Sara and she said, "This is the form from the court verifying you have completed your hours of community service. Congratulations." Sara sat with a blank look on her face, not knowing what to say. Jill continued, "I really want to thank you. You've given me a great start on writing out my story. I would love a copy of all the notes you've taken if it would be ok. It would really help me to continue because I can't stop now.

"I owe it to my nieces and other family that have asked me for years to tell the whole story."

Sara sat with her mouth slightly open, at a loss for words. After some time, she stammered, "I....... I didn't know, I mean I wasn't keeping track. Wait! We can't stop. Isn't there a lot more to your story? I mean, weren't you in the camp for about two more years from where we just left off?" Jill smiled and said, "Yes, there's a lot more to my story, but you've completed your obligation and all you have to do is take this paper to the court now, and I guess that means, you're free." Jill laughed at her own remark, but Sara wasn't laughing. Sara said, "No, I can't. I mean, I can take the paper to the court, but I don't want to stop. Can't we continue? I want to help you finish your story." Jill reached across the table and took Sara's hand.

"Sara, I appreciate that, and I can't thank you enough. Being here you have helped me more than you know. I can't make you continue, though, now that you've completed your scheduled service." Sara was already objecting, shaking her head "no" before Jill even finished speaking. "Are you kidding Jill? You aren't making me do anything.

"I *want* to continue until we are finished. I mean unless you don't want me here." Jill squeezed Sara's hand saying, "I would love for you to continue helping me finish my story."

Sara stood to walk around the end of the table, and with tearful eyes she hugged Jill. Sara held on to her for a long time. As she continued to hug her, Sara said in what was almost a near whisper, "Thank you." When she released her hold on Jill, she walked back to the other side of the table, sat down, wiped away her tears and asked, "So, what now?" Jill pondered her answer before saying, "Well you should take this form to the court to show you have completed your service. I'm going to give you a note stating that you have my permission to continue helping me. That way, no one questions us continuing. I insist on talking to your parents and getting their blessing." Sara exclaimed excitedly, "That shouldn't be a problem, and all of that sounds good to me."

Jill placed the completed form back into the folder and handed it to Sara. She said, "I will call your parents later and if it's ok with them, we can continue.

Will next Saturday be, okay?" As Sara drove away, she felt a warmth deep inside that she once again had not felt in a long time.

Chapter 20:

When Jill called Susan and Paul, they were more than pleased to give their blessing for Sara to continue helping with Jill's writing project. Susan's voice broke slightly when she told Jill that for the first in a very long time, she had begun to notice a genuine smile return on Sara's face. She told Jill that she could not thank her enough for helping to bring Sara out of the very dark place she had fallen into. Jill told Susan and Paul they had a precious daughter, and she was happy to know she was doing well. Jill's final words to Susan and Paul were, "Perhaps when the writing of my story is complete, you will have a chance to read it, and then you will understand how much Sara's being here has helped me as well."

As they sat at the table the following Saturday, Jill thought she noticed a dramatic difference in Sara's demeanor, especially compared to the first couple of weekly sessions they had together. Jill noticed that Sara had brought a new notebook and seemed eager to take notes. Jill was the first to speak. "Ok, tell me where we left off and we'll go on." Sara took her other notebook out of her backpack and opened to the last page.

"Ok, you were showing and telling me about those beautiful birthday cards you had kept all these years." Jill said, "Oh yes. Well, those were among the few highlights I suppose. I don't think anyone would say that conditions ever became ideal. To the credit of many that came from the Islands, they really worked hard to make the best of a not-very-good situation.

"I guess the best way to describe our time as a whole is that it went from bad, to better, and then to worse the closer it got to the end of the war. In the beginning though, once people took on different responsibilities to help organize the school and activities, it really helped. Boredom was probably the biggest problem at first. I mentioned before that no one knew what was going to come next, or how long we would be kept there. Anything to take people's minds off the reality of our situation helped at least some.

"Of course, the war continued, but very little real news about it reached those of us in the camp. The war continued all around us as well. Some of the scariest times were the air raids. It wasn't uncommon for us to hear planes in the distance. Sometimes even before we heard the planes, the sirens would blast.

"They could be heard all through the camp and beyond, into the nearby town of Biberach. "There really was nowhere to go to be protected from possible bombing attacks. We would still all scurry into the barracks anyway. We often heard bombs exploding in the distance. So, that was a constant reminder that we were not living a normal life.

"School kept all of us kids busy for parts of the day at least. The adults really worked hard to make the camp a home and a working community. When we started getting the Red Cross packages, the food situation improved. The cans of meat and fish made a big difference. It still wasn't great, but we all made do because the amount each individual or family got still wasn't much. The men were always housed in a separate building, but we were allowed to visit and do things all together during the day. The barracks were locked at night though.

"Every other week, the wives and children would visit with their husbands in their barracks, and the following week the men would visit in the women's and children's barracks. That schedule was actually set up by the committees that organized the camp rules.

341

"We had our own security, or police group that patrolled at night and kept the children from being disruptive during the day. Anything to lessen the involvement of the guards was the goal. A few adults would occasionally get out of control, and at times would even be locked up in a makeshift jail that was set up in one of the buildings in the camp.

"By that first December in 1942 at Biberach, it was clear to everyone that we most likely would not be going back home by Christmas. We had all been in the camp in the Biberach camp for only about a month when Christmas was nearing. In later years, there were men who made toys from pieces of wood, and women who did sewing. They were making new clothes out of any material that might be available, and several women made beautiful little dolls for girls. Things were still getting organized by that first Christmas though, so there were no presents to share among family and friends. The Germans had allowed the camp to bring in a couple of Christmas trees from the town. There were no lights for the trees, but everyone decorated them with a little bit of everything. Sometimes the decorations were just a piece of cloth tied into a bow.

"We used colored paper from the Red Cross packages folded to look like a bird. Just having a tree lifted peoples spirits a little. I was asked one time what my oldest Christmas memory was. My answer was an event from that first Christmas at Biberach.

"My father was able to come to our barracks to spend the afternoon with us there. "He had the Red Cross package that had been given to us. As we sat around the table, he slowly opened the package. He started pulling items out of the box.

"He placed a can of milk on the table, then a few other things. He smiled as he pulled an orange from the box. My eyes widened, and I stretched as far as I could to see if there were more oranges, but the box was empty. I sat back down and I'm sure I wore a frown on my face. He held the orange for a moment, just staring at it. Then he handed it over to my mother. She took it in her hands as if was a delicate piece of glassware or figurine. She stared at it and then brought it up towards her face with both hands. I watched as she closed her eyes. She brought it to her nose and slowly drew in a breath, and held it in.

"She still had her eyes closed as she moved the orange over slightly and held it against her cheek. She lowered her hands, opened her eyes, and continued to stare at it for a bit. She turned towards me and handed me the orange. I took the orange and did the same thing I had seen her do. I held it up to my nose and sniffed to see if I remembered what one smelled like.

"My father held out his hand and I started to hand it back to him but pulled my hand back at the last second. He smiled and motioned for me to give it to him. I laughed, and without saying anything I handed it across the table to him. He turned to my mother saying, "Shall we?" She simply nodded without saying anything. I watched as Father slowly peeled the orange. He took his time pulling small pieces of the peel off and laying them on the table. My mother gathered up the pieces as he sat each one down. She used the peels later to add some flavoring to drinks or something, but I don't remember exactly what. Very little of anything was thrown away if you could think of another use for it.

"When my father had finished, he held the orange in his hand again and turned it from side to side as if examining it for flaws.

"He maybe was just admiring the beauty of it. When you are in situations like we were in, it's easy to find beauty in the simplest things.

"He pulled at the center and then began separating the small wedges apart. He first handed one to my mother, then to me and my brother. I think I made that first wedge last four bites, taking small, tiny ones so it would last. There were two wedges of the orange for each of us. When I was down to the last bite of my second wedge, I chewed it for so long, there eventually wasn't anything left of it. "I savored it almost like a piece of hard candy that finally disappears when it dissolves in your mouth.

"It's one of those little things that stays way in the back of your mind, like a sound, or in this case, a smell and a taste that jogs a distant memory. That's my oldest Christmas memory, the time our family got one orange for Christmas.

"After that Christmas, Mary and I went out to play. There was quite a bit of snow on the ground, and as usual, it was really cold. We were playing in the snow, throwing an occasional snowball at each other and laughing hysterically.

"Sometimes I would notice the guards watching us play like that, and they would have a smile on their face. I wonder now if they were thinking about their own children back home. I imagine some of them wondered if they would ever even see their families again.

"One of those days when we were playing out in the snow, Mother opened the door of the barracks and called for us to come over. She handed each of us a cup, and then she put a spoonful of condensed milk in each one, cheerfully saying, 'Add some snow to that and stir it up and you'll have ice cream.' We smiled and ran off to make our treat. We did as mom had told us, stirring snow in the cups. We kept adding more snow when we would get near the bottom of the cup until I'm sure we were just eating snow. Eventually our lips were numb, and we ran back inside."

Chapter 21:

"Spring, and then summer could not come soon enough. I didn't remember ever being in a place that was so cold. I don't think I ever felt completely warm during the winter months. The barracks had a little heat, but it was never enough. Even though it was freezing, me and Mary would still play outside. We would throw snowballs at each other and walk around the building, but we really weren't allowed to go any further or just walk wherever we wanted. The camp was large, and it wasn't that we would have gotten lost, but there was still the reality of armed soldiers walking around and guarding the gates. I sometimes would just stand and stare at the men up in the guard towers. Sometimes one would give a little smile and a wave, but they all seemed so serious and stern most of the time. Mary and I would keep playing until our hands and cheeks were bright red from the cold. We would go back inside and hold our face and hands as close to the heaters as we could without burning ourselves.

"By summer, the camp had started receiving some things from the YMCA, I think from Switzerland. The camp actually received some instruments.

"That's when they formed the camp orchestra, I told you about. There were some costumes in the crate that was delivered to the camp and with those available, some of the adults created a theatre group. Some of the costumes were used to make other clothing for us as well. I remember going to the first show at the camp. I didn't really understand much of the plot of the play, but it was fun doing something different for a change. I remember going to the shows the band would put on, too.

"I think it was the second summer in 1944 when the camp commandant allowed us to put on a parade. We had makeshift floats decorated with things made from anything that people could find. People made costumes, and the procession marched around the camp while the band played, leading the parade. One man even dressed up as Uncle Sam. It surprised a lot of people in the camp that the Germans didn't complain or make us stop. By that time, news had made its way to all the detainees that the United States had entered the war. The Germans were not typically happy about any overt expressions of patriotism towards our homeland or the allies.

Biberach Camp Orchestra

"I'm sure a lot of the guards around our camp felt like babysitters. Not many people in the camp were interested in starting trouble, honestly. The adults who had been put in charge of keeping everyone organized in the camp had done a pretty good job. I think after it became clear we were all going to be there for a very long time, everyone just kind of went through the motions of the daily routine. That's why things like the band performance were such a welcome distraction. We were even allowed to have dances. Me and Mary would just sit along the wall and watch all the adults; we didn't really dance ourselves. I can't really remember the first time I actually danced in my life.

"At one point the commandant of the camp started allowing escorted walks outside the camp for exercise. Escorted meant with guards walking with us, always carrying their guns. It seemed strange to walk around the little town of Biberach, only to have to go back behind the barbed wire fences, locked away again in the prison we had come to call home. We would walk down the street and most times, people would just stare at us, especially other kids. I always used to silently ask myself what those German kids thought about us.

"As the war went on, basic supplies became hard for even the German citizens to get, so people from the camp would save some of the items from the Red Cross packages for the townspeople. The guards would more or less turn their back when my mother and others would trade things to the locals. Sometimes they would trade cigarettes and other items for fresh vegetables, clothing, or other things that we wanted or needed. I learned later on in life, and after reading what happened throughout Germany,

"Many of the German citizens didn't have it much better off than we did as far as having enough food and other essentials.

"I had mentioned before that my father did dental work on the guards and other people. After a while, my father was allowed outside the camp on certain days to perform dental work on the local residents. In one of the empty offices in a building inside the camp, he would help other prisoners and any of the guards that needed it. This was something that ended up probably saving my life.

Guard tower at internment camp

Chapter 22:

"There was one particular guard named Hans Hauschild. My father had done some dental work on him. I'm not exactly sure of the extent of the work he did, but Hans was very grateful and actually became friends with my father. At least as much of a friendship that would have been allowed between a German soldier and one of the internment camp prisoners. Hans would stop and talk to me and Mary when we would be outside playing. Sometimes if we had a piece of hard candy from one of the Red Cross packages, we would give him one. He always smiled and would tell us in German, 'Dankeschön'. Then in heavily accented English he would say, "Thank you." He would rub the top of our heads and smile before going on his way.

"By now it had been more than two years since we were taken from Guernsey. I can't say that the time went by fast, but I was now ten years old, and I remember many more things than when I was only six and the Germans first came to Guernsey. It was now 1944, and the war for us had been going on for more than four full years. Going into the winter, things began to get gradually worse.

"Food shortages became the biggest concern. Just getting firewood or whatever else to heat our barracks became more and more hard to get too. We already were wearing two or more layers of clothes just to keep warm. I was still too young to realize the significance, but the fact that supplies were becoming harder to get, was a sign that things were not going well for the Germans in the war effort.

"During the winter, I almost always had at least a slight cold. Sometimes the outside of my nose would be raw from having constant sniffles. One morning I woke up with my throat hurting. I had had sore throats before during the colder months, but this time, my throat felt raw, and it hurt to swallow. In the previous two years, we had some medicines available in the camp, but like everything else there wasn't much in the way of medicine to help with a sore throat. My mother warmed up some tea. It's hard to call it "tea" as the tea leaves had been used up to the point where they barely colored the water. It warmed me inside though, as I took small sips, and it felt good on my sore throat.

"The sore throat persisted, and by the third day it hurt worse.

"My father looked down my throat, shook his head sympathetically, and commented that it was very red and swollen. Father told my mother to keep me as warm as possible and to keep me inside. I didn't really want to go outside anyway, because by that third day of constant pain in my throat, I felt sicker than just a sore throat. Now I was feeling more like a bad flu. I had no energy, was constantly blowing my nose, and my throat was not getting better. I had a slight fever, but by the fourth day the fever had gotten worse.

"I lay in my bed all day, and every once in a while, my mother would wipe my face and forehead with a damp cloth. If there was any relief from that, it never lasted more than a few seconds. I was really weak and just wanted to sleep all day, but it hurt so much to swallow, that even that made it hard to fall asleep.

"I remember on the morning of the fifth day, my mother seemed more worried than she had previously. She felt my forehead and I was burning up. I don't know how high my fever actually was, but I'm sure it was well over 100. My mother's hand felt ice-cold, even though her hand was probably room-temperature.

"Another lady that lived in the barracks came over when my mother called for her, and she felt my forehead too. I coughed, and it felt like needles were stabbing the sides of my throat inside, and I couldn't swallow hardly at all. When I coughed, I would groan and try not to cry, but I could feel tears slowly running down the side of my face. Mother would wipe them away with a cloth, and I'd close my eyes and drift off again. I might have even been kind of going in and out of consciousness at that point because I was so weak.

"While lying in bed with my eyes closed, I could hear voices, several different voices, and one of them was my father. I could hear my mother talking to him but wasn't able to really understand what she was saying. I opened my eyes only about halfway and remember seeing my father looking down at me. He touched his hand to my cheek, then turned to my mother and said something. He had a concerned look on his face but that's all I remember. My head hurt really bad and there was a ringing in my ears that made it hard to hear most of what anyone around me was saying. He put his hand on my forehead and before I closed my eyes, I saw him turn and walk away.

"I would find out much later that my father went outside looking for Hans, the German guard. He told Han's that his daughter was very sick and needed help. My father then brought Hans to the barracks.

"I opened my eyes again when I heard several voices. The faint light in the room still hurt my eyes, and that made the ringing in my ears and the headache worse. Someone touched my forehead, maybe it was Hans, but I really wasn't sure because I kept my eyes closed. It just hurt too much to keep them open.

"I must have been awake some of the rest of the afternoon, but I really don't remember. My fever stayed high. I knew that because whether I was awake or half-asleep, my mother kept wiping my forehead. My mother had tried to get me to drink broth of some kind, but my throat would hurt so much trying to swallow that I would spit the broth back out. My throat felt like it was closed when I would try to swallow.

"The rest of that afternoon and into the evening was a blur. I would wake up when I coughed because of the pain it would cause in my throat. I don't know what time it was, but my mother woke me up in the middle of the night and said she was going to help me get dressed.

"She helped raise me up, but I didn't have any energy to help her. She wrapped a scarf around my throat and put my coat on me. She wrapped a blanket around me and then I saw my father and Hans, the guard walk into our barracks. There were two other small boys with Hans. I didn't understand what was happening.

"My father took my hand, bent down close to me and told me, 'Hans is going to take you where someone can help you.' All I could do was nod my head slightly. My father picked me up and handed me over to Hans. When they carried me outside, all I knew was that it was nighttime because it was completely dark. I saw snow on the ground, and even though I was bundled up pretty good, I could still feel the icy cold air on my face.

"The wind was blowing a little, and Hans reached up and pulled the blanket over my head. I could see out of the blanket a little bit and I noticed that we had come to the gate. I don't know if it was Hans or someone else who did it, but the gate opened, and we walked out of the camp. The fact that we were doing this at night, and maybe with the cooperation of another guard confirmed my thoughts - Hans was sneaking us out of the camp.

Chapter 23:

"The ground was covered with fresh snow, and I could hear the crunch of gravel under Hans' feet as he walked. He would occasionally say something to the two boys that were walking beside him. It wasn't long before we left what seemed like a main road, and I could see down below that this new road or path hadn't been walked or driven on since it filled with snow. Every so often, Hans would shift me to his other arm. I was 10 years old now, so it must have been difficult for him to carry me. I was too weak to walk by myself, though, and we continued down a pathway through the woods. A few times, Hans stopped to rest on the stump of a tree for a few moments and then we would continue. I struggled in the cold even though I was bundled up in everything my mother could find. I was burning up with fever, and yet I couldn't stop shivering.

"There was more snow falling now, but it seemed like the wind had died down. We came to a stone gate where the road or driveway sloped up. I remember Hans' grunting, probably from exhaustion as we walked up the hill. I don't know what building we had arrived at, was but it seemed large.

"When Hans knocked on the door, a lady dressed all in white opened it and motioned for us to come in. Hans sat me down on a chair next to a wood stove, and the two boys sat on the floor warming their hands close to the stove. Hans sat across the room talking to the lady that had let us in, but I couldn't hear what he was saying. The lady left the room and came back with three other ladies. They all gathered around Hans talking, and they kept looking over at me and the boys. Finally, one of the ladies came over, and in German she said something to the boys and motioned for them to follow her. They stood up and held hands, following the lady out of the room. Seeing the ladies all dressed in white, I still to this day don't know if we were at a hospital with nurses helping us, or perhaps at a convent and these were nuns.

"Another lady had come into the room to talk to Hans. One of the ladies in white came over to me and gently took the blanket off my shoulders. She felt my forehead and drew her hand back, seemingly startled. She said something rapidly in German to the other two ladies. "They all three turned to Hans, and he nodded. I guess he was giving them the ok to do whatever it was the lady had said."

"At that point, Jill paused her story. When Sara looked up from her notebook, she saw that Jill looked slightly pale. "Are you ok Jill?" Jill shook her head a little as though she had been daydreaming and suddenly heard something that snapped her out of it. "I'm sorry," Jill replied, "I would just like to take a break for a bit if that's ok. I'm going to get something to drink, and then we'll continue." Jill came back to the table shortly afterward and sat down.

"I'm sorry Sara, this part of my story is one that I both think about and try not to think about as well. It was a scary time. Even with everything that had happened to all of us up to that point, this was probably the scariest thing of all that I had went through. So, it's been a little hard talking about it." It was Sara's turn now to reach across the table and put her hand on Jill's and reassure, "It's alright, I'm sure I understand. We can stop for today if you want." Jill shook her head. "No, we can get through this part of the story and then stop. In for a penny, in for a pound as they say." Then Jill gave her a strained looking smile.

"Jill took a sip from her glass and continued. "I never heard what was wrong with the two boys.

"They walked the whole way themselves, so I assume they weren't as bad off as I was. I don't know where the lady had taken them, or what she was doing with them. I only assume that they were sick also, but I don't know with what.

"Hans walked over and put his arms under my legs to pick me up. He carried me across the room and followed the ladies through the door and down a long hallway. One of the ladies spoke some English, turning to me saying, "We will make you better." When Hans sat me back down in a chair, the lady sat down and reached over to feel my forehead, softly saying, "kleines Mädchen" which means 'little girl'. She touched her fingers to my throat and in an even tone said, 'Your tonsils are very swollen and infected. I must take them out.'"

"I didn't really understand exactly what she was saying, but I nodded my head up and down anyway. She brushed the matted hair away from my forehead and said in English, 'We do not have any way to numb your throat, or anesthesia to make you sleep while we do it. Do you understand?' "I just stared at her because I didn't really understand.

"She raised my chin, so I was looking directly at her when she said, 'I'm sorry, it's going to be very painful. It will hurt much.' Then she nodded as if she was willing me to understand.

"Then the other two ladies lined up some chairs and sat down. The lady who had talked to me began giving them directions, and Hans laid me down across the two ladies' laps. The lady in charge had her chair turned sideways to the other ladies, and she took my head and laid it down in her lap. In that position, she was upside-down when I looked up at her. I looked around the room, but all I remember seeing was the clock on the wall. Then the lady put her hands on both sides of my head and pulled it back slightly. One of the other ladies put something in my mouth. I don't know if it was metal or wood, but it kept me from closing my mouth. One lady held my legs down, and the other leaned over and held my arms tight against my sides. The lady with my head in her lap pulled a metal cart over beside her. She spread her legs slightly, so my head dropped a little, then she squeezed the inside of her legs against my head tight like a vise.

"I was scared, and I tried to swallow but couldn't. I remember looking in her eyes, and the next thing I knew, I saw in her hand some type of scissors or other cutting device. She didn't hesitate as she pressed the fingers of one hand in my mouth, holding it open as far as it would go. I thought the corners of my mouth were going to split. I gagged as she reached into my mouth with the tool she had. I gagged again and screamed as she cut my tonsils. I remember the pain and screaming, but then I passed out, thankfully."

Sara put her hand to her mouth in horror, then bolted into the kitchen and almost threw up over the sink. She gagged a couple of times but managed to hold off. She turned the water on so she could splash some on her face. She hadn't noticed Jill had come into the kitchen behind her. Jill placed a hand on Sara's shoulder and handed her a towel. Sara turned, took the towel and buried her head into Jill's shoulder as her arms went around to hug her tight. Jill could feel Sara's shoulders shaking slightly and knew she was crying. Jill patted Sara's head and just held her.

Chapter: 24

After nearly a full minute, Sara backed away and wiped her face with the towel. She held the towel against her face for a bit and then finally looked up at Jill. "I'm so sorry, I…." Jill held her hand up to let Sara know not to worry. "I'm sorry, I should maybe have warned you how graphic this part of the story was going to be. Do you want to stop for the day?" Sara shook her head. "No, I'm ok. Tell me what happened next at least, and then we can break for the day."

They sat back down at the table. Jill took a deep breath and started right in. "I had said that thankfully I had passed out. When I woke up, I remember looking over at the clock and it had been an hour since I last saw what time it was. I probably had gone into shock or something. I had been out for a whole hour. My throat hurt terribly, but not a whole lot different than the sharp needle-like pain from before when I would swallow.

"The difference now was that it was more concentrated in one area, I guess where my tonsils had been cut out, and the pain was constant, not just when I tried to swallow."

Sara shuddered just thinking about what Jill had gone through. Sara shook her head back and forth saying, "I'm so sorry, I can't even imagine. I don't want to try and imagine." Jill nodded and gave Sara a thankful smile. "Well, it probably saved my life, so I'm thankful for that. When I woke up, I was wrapped back in the blanket again.

"I never knew what was wrong with those boys that had come with us, but they were back and sitting on the floor by the wood stove. Hans was talking with the ladies, but I couldn't hear what they were saying. Hans came over to me saying in broken English, 'Come, we go now.' I tried to stand, and my knees almost gave way, but Hans scooped me up like before and cradled my head against his shoulder. The air seemed even colder than before as we went outside. This time though, it actually made my throat feel better when I would breathe in the cold air through my mouth. The boys were following but Hans had to keep motioning for them to hurry along.

"It was still snowing lightly, and it was still the middle of the night, but I had no idea what time it was. We walked for a while when Hans suddenly stopped.

"He had seen something on the side of the road. It was an old baby stroller, but it still had wheels that would roll. Hans put one of the boys in the stroller and the other one stood on the back, and somehow Hans pushed the two boys on the stroller while still carrying me. The man must have had a back and shoulders made of steel. After about an hour of traveling, I looked up and saw the outline of the camp up ahead. As we approached, someone opened the gate, and we went through.

"Hans knocked on the door of our barracks and someone opened the door but I'm not sure who it was. I remember being placed back on my bed, and I heard muffled, but excited voices, but I drifted off to sleep. At some point, I woke up and it was daylight outside. My mother was standing across the room at the table, talking with other ladies when she noticed I had opened my eyes. She rushed over and put her hand on my forehead. She put her hands on both sides of my face and smiled. The fever had almost immediately started going down once the infected tonsils were taken out, and now was almost completely gone. She told me not to try to talk, and then put a cup with cool water to my mouth and I drank a small amount. The water felt good, but it still hurt terribly to swallow.

"It took several days but eventually the pain was just like a regular sore throat.

"My mother told me it would take a few days before I could probably have solid food. I didn't have stitches where they had cut my tonsils out, but I'm not sure how they closed the wound to keep it from bleeding. Each day my throat felt better, but those first few days I only had soup broth, warm tea, and water.

"I will never forget Hans, the man that took a chance, possibly with his own life to sneak me out of the camp and carry me through the countryside in the dark of the night. He almost certainly saved my life. Years later, I had the privilege of meeting Hans again, along with his wife when they visited the United States. I was able to show them around San Francisco and spend a day or two with them. That was the last time I saw or talked to Hans. I unfortunately do not have any pictures of Hans. I wish I did, but he will forever be in my mind." As Jill made her last statement, she choked back some tears and dabbed her eyes with a tissue.

When she looked across the table, Sara was sitting spellbound, her mouth half open, tears coursing down her cheeks.

They sat just looking at each other for a long time. Finally, Sara spoke. "I'm just in shock at what you went through." Jill laughed lightly, responding, "The funny thing is, later I had to have my tonsils removed again. I don't know if maybe the nurses or nuns had only removed part of my tonsils or what, but whatever it was that they did, I have no doubt it saved my life because I had been suffering with that high fever for 5 days and I may not have been able to fight for much longer. At the time I had been sick with the fever and went through what I just described, the war was rapidly deteriorating for Germany, and things were getting very worrisome around the camp. Of course, we didn't know it at the time. but there were only a few months remaining in the war, and those final months in some ways were the worst of all for us."

Jill appeared contemplative and didn't say anything else for quite some time. It seemed that their visit had reached a natural conclusion, at least for that day. Jill reached across and placed her hand once again on top of Sara's hand. "Well Sara, we're getting close to the end. Well at least the end of this chapter of my life." She patted Sara's hand and squeezed it affectionately.

"Thank you, Sara. Thank you for being such a good listener."

Chapter 25:

Sara sat on the bench looking at Robert's grave. "I'm feeling better these days, Robert." A tear ran down her cheek and she gently wiped it away. "For a long time, I kept telling myself I didn't deserve to feel good or happy anymore because that wasn't fair. If you couldn't be here and go on with your life, then why should I be allowed to just go on with mine? My heart still aches for you, Robert. I don't think that will ever stop, but I know you wouldn't want that to consume me. I still catch myself walking by the door to your bedroom, and imagining I can just stop and knock on the door to hear you say, 'Is that you, dork? Come on in.' I'll open the door and there you'll be, sitting on your bed reading or studying, and you'll close your books and say, 'What's up?' That was you, Robert. No matter what you were doing, if someone needed something, you stopped whatever you were doing and were ready to help. Especially for me.

"You would pat your hand on the bed for me to join you. I would sit down, and you would just sit there not saying anything. You always knew that I eventually would gather my thoughts.

"Then I would start telling you what was going on. You were so much more mature than me, and always had the right words to help.

"I'm sorry, Robert." Sara choked up and her tears flowed freely now as she continued, sobbing between her words. "I'm sorry for being angry at you. You didn't deserve that. You would have been there for me if the roles had been reversed. I know that in my heart. You would have been the strong one, I know that for sure. Now, instead of me being strong for you, I closed myself off from everyone. The worst thing was, I distanced myself from you. You were suffering and I wasn't there for you." She wept uncontrollably as she said, "Please forgive me Robert, please."

She felt a hand on her shoulder just then but wasn't even shocked or surprised. Her dad had joined her, and he sat down next to her quietly. She turned and fell into his arms. He held her as she wept silently for a while. Paul said after a moment, "How about we go get some ice cream." Sara looked up at her father as he handed her a handkerchief. She wiped her eyes and after composing herself, said pleadingly, "I'm sorry Daddy." Fresh tears came as she pressed her face to his shoulder.

Paul held his daughter tightly without saying anything for a while. He patted Sara's back and said, "I'm sorry, sweetheart. I wish I could have done more for Robert and for you. The one thing I know for sure is that Robert wouldn't want us to not go on with our lives. When I first said that to myself some time ago, I thought how selfish I was being. I know it's true, though. Robert cared about other people, especially his kid sister, and he would be heartbroken if you changed from the person, you were when he was still here." Sara had composed herself by then, and looked at her father, and simply nodded her head in agreement. Paul gave her a final hug, saying, "Now how about that ice cream?"

That next week Sara began taking her studies more seriously and for the first time in a long while, she felt like she might actually be ok. She went to Jill's house the following weekend with new confidence. When she walked in, Jill noticed a change as well. "You look good Sara." Jill remarked. Sara smiled. "Hmmm, well you know what Jill? I feel good. Let's start right away if that's ok. I really want to hear what happened next."

They sat down at the table and Sara saw that Jill had some items laid out on the table. Sara picked up a book and read the title out loud, "A Child's War". Jill began, "I thought I would show you some good research material…if you are interested in looking further into the history. Molly Bihet wrote this book about her experiences, and it's an excellent account of the occupation of the island and then her time in Biberach." She showed Sara a few other items, a DVD set of a British drama series, and a couple other books. Jill took a deep breath before saying, "Well, shall we continue?"

Chapter 26:

Jill began, "The last thing I mentioned when we finished up last week was that around the time I had the ordeal with my tonsils, there were only about four months left in the war. Of course, as I mentioned, we didn't know it at the time.

"I think a lot of the adults were starting to really worry if it was just inevitable that we were never going to make it back to our homes alive." Sara interrupted and said, "Yes, and you said that in some ways it was the worst time for all of you. How was it worse if you knew you were going to get to go home soon?"

Jill blew out a muddled sigh, saying, "Well that's the thing, like I said, we didn't know. The Red Cross parcels had stopped arriving, and food rations were even more scarce than when we had first arrived almost three years earlier. In those final months, the actual fighting had gotten much closer to where we were in Biberach. The feeling around the camp was that the Germans were rapidly losing ground, and although we believed the Allies would win, would they do it in time to save us all?

"I read later accounts where some adults in our camp halfway expected the Germans to kill all their prisoners. I guess in retaliation - or just let us all starve. So, the feeling around the camp was uneasiness. We didn't know whether we would survive to eventually be liberated.

"For weeks, we could hear bombs way off in the distance. It was a daily thing, and it seemed like it was almost non-stop. Probably only about a month after my ordeal with having my tonsils out, we began to experience air raids. The sirens would go off and we would be quickly huddled into our barracks. The explosions were getting closer every day, and it wasn't much longer till we actually would see American and British airplanes flying over on bombing raids. There was a constant state of fear in the camp during that time. All of the regular activities had stopped pretty much, and everyone seemed to be just in a mindset of survival. Everyone was hoping and praying those planes knew we were in this camp so they wouldn't bomb us.

"One of the worst things during that time is that as the Germans were losing ground, they started evacuating some of the camps.

"At one point, there was a large group of Jewish prisoners moved into our camp.

"The look of these people when they got to our camp are images that you could never get out of your mind. You could tell they had all been extremely abused, probably beaten on a regular basis. They were marched in wearing tattered clothes, and some didn't even have shoes on. Their faces were gaunt, their eyes sunken in, and their bones stuck out from being almost starved to death. They were housed in other buildings, not ours.

"Quite a few died in the camp there at Biberach right after they arrived. I have no doubt many more died even after the liberation of the camp because they were just too weak to ever recover totally. The sight of those Jewish people really confirmed what the English had thought about the Germans all along, that at least those that were in power, - represented pure evil."

"Another day would pass with more air raids. At the beginning of April 1945, our food supplies were next to nothing. There were many days where we had nothing but a little bit of broth that was so watered down, it was almost like drinking just warm water. There was no meat of any kind anymore.

"We occasionally would still get one of the moldy loaves of bread that we would have to pick the bugs out of before we could eat it. There was no butter or jam anymore. I guess we learned what the term, 'living on bread and water' really meant.

"There were no more walks allowed outside the camp, but I was at least allowed outside the barracks. Mary and I would stand along the fence of the camp looking towards the town, and it seemed almost deserted. I guess maybe a lot of people had left, sensing that the war was getting closer to them, and they had better leave while they could.

"One day, one of the scariest moments happened since we had come to Biberach. I was outside the barracks, probably with Mary as usual. There was a plane flying overhead. That wasn't unusual during this time, but something seemed different with this one. This plane must have had some type of problem. I had read later that part of the plane had actually come off in flight, and the pilot couldn't control it anymore.

"The plane came down and we could hear the engine really loud. I think everyone thought it would crash in the camp and people were screaming and running.

"We don't know if the pilot was trying to keep from hitting the camp, but he might have been. The plane swooshed overhead.

"At the last second it just barely cleared one of the barracks buildings and the outer fence of the camp, then crashed just beyond the fence. The plane exploded and it was deafening. It was a horrible sound and shook the ground where I was standing. I think back and imagine, it's just another one of those things a little girl should never have had to experience.

"It seemed that every day the sounds of the bombs exploding were getting closer and closer. Mom made me stay inside the barracks almost all day long now. Some news had gotten through to the camp: the allies were pushing the Germans further back every day, and the Germans were also sustaining heavy losses. The reports kept saying it was just a matter of time before the final victory would be had. For all of us though, everyone I'm sure was thinking, "Would the victory come soon enough?"

"It wasn't long before we started seeing British and American planes flying over. They were pretty high up, and thankfully, they weren't dropping bombs.

"I guess they were doing daily flights to look at what was happening on the ground with the German forces.

"Whenever people were outside their barracks and would see the planes, you could hear cheers go up around the camp. Most of the guards had stopped trying to squelch things like that. I'm sure most of them were thinking more about their own survival.

"By the following week, the planes were flying lower, and the bombs seemed like they were only a few miles away. Then one day, the air raid siren went off and we were all huddled in our barracks when a bomb exploded in town. That explosion shook the ground throughout the entire camp. I remember some of the women were crying, and some I could hear praying softly. That's one of the first times I remember the war and everything that had happened making me feel afraid. I was old enough now to understand the destruction those bombs caused, and that if one went off near us or especially on our barracks, we most likely would not survive.

Chapter 27:

"The planes began bombing the town of Biberach for several days, and every one of the bombs shook the ground around us. We thought it was just a matter of time before they bombed our camp and that would be it. Then one day around the middle of April, it happened. A bomb had hit one of our buildings. Fortunately, it wasn't one of the barracks, it was a supply building or something. We never found out if it was a mistake, or maybe a stray bomb that had missed its original intended target. After the bombing stopped, people went outside and saw the building that was destroyed. I remember everyone just standing and staring at the building, or what was left of it, and not saying anything. The war had come inside the camp.

"That week, the German guards started making everyone stay inside our barracks. We would still look out the windows and try to see what was happening. Around the beginning of the third week of April, there were a lot of trucks and other vehicles leaving the camp with German soldiers in them. We didn't know really what was happening. We realized eventually they were in the process of abandoning the camp.

"They were fleeing Biberach and moving further away from what had become the front lines.

"On April 22nd, word came that the Allies were only about a mile from the town. We saw what seemed like hundreds of planes flying over us now. Everyone worried that if the allies came into town, they wouldn't realize the place we were at was a prisoner of war camp, and they would start firing on everyone. The adults started grabbing anything that was white and began hanging makeshift white flags on the fences, doorways, poles, anything they could attach one to. Someone even hung a flag from Guernsey on one of the barracks.

"The next day, April 23rd, my father came running into our barracks and said he had heard the Allied troops were coming and were very close. There were still sounds of bombs and now even gunfire now nearby. We hadn't heard the gunfire sounds up until that point because individual fighting hadn't been that close to us. Most of the Germans had fled our camp by that day but for some reason a few had stayed behind.

"We were outside, in hopes that the soldiers and the planes would see that we weren't Germans and decide not to fire at us or drop more bombs on the camp.

"We heard and then felt a rumbling sound. Then we saw it, a tank coming towards the camp. I couldn't tell if it was German or not. I was standing with Mary, and she reached over and took my hand. We looked at each other but didn't say anything. The tank came within about 50 meters of the fence surrounding the camp and just stopped. There was an eerie silence that followed then. The only sound being that of the low rumbling idle of the tank as it sat facing the camp. I guess everyone was just waiting to see what was going to happen next. Would it fire into the camp or not?

"Then something happened that I will never forget. Two German guards that had remained behind and were up in one of the guard towers along the fence of the camp pointed their rifles at the tank. Those two guards foolishly started firing their rifles. I could hear the pinging sound of the bullets bouncing off the armor of the tank.

"I remember opening my eyes wide as I saw the top of the tank start turning. It was turning towards where the guard tower was. When it stopped, the barrel of the huge gun started raising up. Then there was a puff of smoke from the barrel.

"That was immediately followed by the loudest sound I had ever heard. I could see everything as if it were in slow motion. The puff of smoke, what looked like a flame from the end of the tank's gun, and then the tower exploded. It was like Poof! It was just gone. It lay in a pile of rubble, and of course there was no sign of the two guards that had been inside. I guess the fortunate thing for them was it was a quick death. Why they hadn't just surrendered, I'll never understand. Maybe they were so scared seeing the tank approaching that they couldn't think straight, and just fired their rifles. Whatever their thinking was, it was the wrong thought.

"Mary and I felt the force of the explosion vibrate through our bodies, and we jumped back in terror. More tanks came into view along with some other vehicles. It ended up that they were French troops and vehicles, because the Americans had allowed the French to come in first and liberate the camp.

"The adults started running and yelling, and waving pieces of anything white they could find. They had to let the French troops know that those of us left in the camp weren't the Germans.

"Next, trucks pulled up to the front gate of the camp, and soldiers jumped out with their guns pointed towards all of us. Several of the men approached the gate with their hands up and waving the white flags they had made.

"I remember I was starting to have a hard time breathing. I was shaking, and Mary and I hugged each other. My lower lip was quivering, and I wasn't sure if it was out of fear or anticipation. A French officer approached the gate, and two of the soldiers with him unlatched the gate and swung it open. There were a few seconds of total silence, and then the officer yelled, "You are free!"

"I began to sob uncontrollably and thought I was going to collapse. I was thankful that Mary and I were still holding on to each other. People started screaming and hollering in celebration, and the French officer was mobbed with hugs and kisses. The vehicles and soldiers started moving into the camp, and everyone was talking to the soldiers, asking them questions about the war. I heard my name and turned to see my mother and Mary's mother coming towards us. They each took us in their arms and hugged us.

"It was another one of the few affectionate moments I really remember with my mother.

"The Americans came into the camp next. I remember some of the American troops gave us rides in their jeeps and gave us chewing gum. There was a real sense of celebration all around us. I remember thinking we would be going home the next day. The war was still going on, though, so it wasn't as if we could just pack up and head for home. Officially, the war lasted another two weeks.

"It was said that on April 30th, that Hitler committed suicide. Then on May 7th, the Germans on the western front surrendered unconditionally. On May 9th, the remainder of the German forces on the eastern front surrendered to the Soviets. It would still be a full month from that April 23rd day before we started being moved out of the camp.

"I was still too young to understand everything, but I can imagine now the logistics once the war was officially over had to be a nightmare, moving prisoners back to their home countries. Not only the more than 2000 citizens from the islands but thousands of POW's.

"On that April 23rd day, it had been 4 years, 9 months, and 24 days since the Germans had first arrived in Guernsey. Almost five full years of my young life. I wasn't the little girl I had been when I first heard that snapping of the jackbooted soldiers marching through the streets of Guernsey.

Liberation Day in Biberach

Chapter 28:

"The French and the Americans started bringing in supplies, and we finally had plenty of food again. The first to leave the camp right away were the Jewish prisoners, many who were already near death. When they finally started moving all of the rest of us out, they went in alphabetical order. So, with our name being Pay, we were near the last group to be moved out. One day while we were still waiting for the day we would get to leave; my father and I took a walk outside the camp. I remember seeing bombed-out buildings all over the town. I wondered how many people in town had died in those bombings, or if they had all gotten out of town in time. There were a couple of scraggly-looking dogs rummaging for food, I guess, and a few other animals just wandering around the streets.

"We walked down to the river. I remember the air was still very chilly, but it didn't matter to me. It was the first time we had walked outside of the camp without armed German soldiers watching over us. We sat on a rock at the edge of the river, and I took my shoes and socks off and put my feet in the water. It was icy cold, but all I could do was giggle.

"I looked up towards the sky and squinted from the sunlight. My dad put his arm around me and pulled me close. He squeezed me a little tighter and held me like that for a while. I looked over at him, and he was just staring across the river. I don't think he was looking at anything in particular, and then in almost a whisper I heard him say, "We're going home. We're really going home.

"I don't remember the exact date, but we finally were told we would be the next to leave. We had already packed up the few personal items we were taking with us. I had kept my handmade greeting cards that had been given to me, as well as the tapestry I had stitched on the piece of burlap. That was about all I was taking back; other than a few clothes my mother had packed. We loaded into some military trucks, and this time none of us had that fear of "where were these soldiers taking us?" Nothing like the feeling we had nearly three years before when we were loaded onto boats, trucks, and trains that began our internment ordeal.

"It took maybe 45 minutes to arrive at an airfield that was about 40 kilometers from Biberach. There we boarded a Royal Airforce Dakota airplane.

"We were finally leaving Germany. We flew from there to Hendon, England, just north of London.

"It was a military plane, so it was nothing like flying in a modern passenger jet. It was noisy and cold but that didn't matter - we were heading home. We landed at the military base in Hendon. It was still a process once we arrived there, but we were finally back on British soil, and we couldn't wait until we got to travel back to Guernsey. It took about two more months before all of our paperwork was processed. After three months from when the French first arrived at the camp in Biberach, we were finally heading home to Guernsey.

"Over the weeks after arriving in Hendon, different groups were transported back to the island they called home. Eventually, we boarded a bus in Hendon and traveled about an hour to the coast. As we traveled, I looked out the window of the bus at the green countryside and the children playing in the fields and in their yards. I thought, 'How different from what I've had to look at for the last three years.'

"We arrived at a port, I'm not sure what town it was. We carried our few belongings onto a small ship, I believe it was a mail ship or boat.

"I remember thinking what a stark difference from the last time we boarded a boat to cross the channel waters. When we were herded into that dirty, overcrowded ship, and the horrible experience of that trip. One difference was we were allowed to be up on the deck as we sailed across the channel. There was definitely a sense of anticipation and excitement. It was July, the sky was clear, and the air was warm for being on the channel. We didn't know what we would find when we got home. The little bits of news we received from back home while we were in the camps didn't really tell us much, and those letters had stopped at least six months before the war ended.

"I don't remember the exact moment I saw the land on the horizon, but a cheer went up from the bow of the boat. People could see the island of Guernsey in the distance, and we all knew that after almost three years, we were almost there. It was two months shy of being three full years since we had last seen our homeland of Guernsey."

Chapter 29:

"As we approached the docks, we could see people cheering and waving flags to welcome us home. I don't remember if anyone in particular welcomed us as we got off the ship, but everyone was hugging and kissing. We eventually were able to get a ride with someone who still had a vehicle. It was about a fifteen-minute ride to Debonair, our house in the country. outside the town. As we pulled up in front of the house, my mother gasped. The plants were overgrown and unkempt. There were broken windows. No one said anything as we took our things and set them on the walk. We stared at the front of the house, then my father moved around me and walked to the front door. We followed him into the house and what we saw was nothing short of depressing.

"There was graffiti on the walls and a few pieces of broken furniture. What furniture that was left intact was piled into one room off the dining room area. It had all been just thrown in a heap. Almost none of the furniture wasn't all scratched up. Our excitement of coming home had quickly turned to despair, and I'm sure anger in my parents.

"We were certain that some of the damage was from the Germans as they began moving out and then off the island. However, there no doubt was damage caused by vandals simply because the house had been left unoccupied and unprotected. It was disappointing to imagine that our fellow islanders would take advantage, but I guess human nature takes over sometimes. Desperate times makes for desperate people.

"My parents did what they could to get the house set up and livable again, but it just wasn't the same. The island itself was still a long way from recovering fully from the war. Most businesses were still closed and there were very few jobs. My father tried to restart his dental practice, but it wasn't long before he realized that there just weren't enough people that could afford dental care to sustain his practice and support our family. My parents eventually made the decision to sell Debonair and move our family to the mainland.

"Our homecoming was bittersweet because we had such high expectations returning to Guernsey. Before being taken away from our home in Guernsey, Debonair was the only home I had known.

"Nothing really memorable happened over the next several weeks. My parents had taken the broken furniture and dishes somewhere, and after cleaning everything up put the house up for sale. It was sold, then the apartment in town was taken care of, and we once again boarded a boat, leaving Guernsey for good this time. People on the Island could no longer afford dental care, so there was nothing left for my father to make a living there. I've been back to visit several times since we left that day, but I never lived there again as my home."

Chapter 30:

"I received quite a surprise when we eventually arrived in Chichester, England, the new place we would call home. That is the first time I found out that my father had a completely separate family, with children even that were much older than me. It took a little while to understand that these children were actually my brothers and sisters. It was a shock and an adjustment. The house was one my father had built for his other family before he met my mother. That's another long story for another time, maybe.

"It was still a strange time, and I wasn't sure how life was supposed to just go on. I hadn't known anything really, other than the time at the camps and the short time when we went back to Guernsey. My parents didn't really know what to do with me. We had some schooling during the time in the camps, but it wasn't sufficient and I'm sure I was behind other kids my age. Eventually, my parents thought the best thing for me was to send me to a boarding school. Of course, you can't compare it to my time in the German camps, but it ended up being four of the worst years of my life. I was miserable the whole time.

"I didn't want to be there. I received an education though, and eventually I returned to Chichester.

"One of my newly found sisters was Enid. It was so nice having a sister, and she showed me what a normal life really could be. We went to the zoo, took walks, and she took me for my first-ever ice cream cone. We became best friends."

Sara had sat silent, rapidly taking notes, and Jill's story was gradually reaching the end. Jill had stopped talking and when Sara finally stopped writing, Jill declared, "Well, Sara, that's pretty much my story. Of course, life went on and I lived my life like everyone else does. I eventually married and had children. We finally decided there was more out there for us, and we immigrated to the United States. My life as an adult has seen some great adventures. My love for the water and boats continued as I mentioned before. And now, after more than 80 years of life, here I am, sitting with you while you help me to tell my story.

"I want to thank you, Sara, for being willing to sit and listen, and I'm looking forward to when you finish putting everything to paper."

Sara closed her notebook, folded her hands together and rested her chin on them. She looked across the table at Jill without saying anything for a moment. "It's me that needs to thank you, Jill.

"You were patient with me in the beginning when it was probably obvious to you that I didn't want to be here. I apologize for anything I might have said or done to show you disrespect. That is not who I am. Well, it isn't who I used to be, but I'm getting back to where I need to be, and I owe a big part of that to you." Jill patted Sara's hand but remained quiet for a while. "I hope this won't be the end of our friendship Sara. I'm looking forward to seeing where you go from here, Sara."

Jill pulled some pictures out of a box and laid them on the table, saying, "These are some pictures I hadn't shown you yet. The one of my sister Enid and me walking with our ice cream cones is one of my favorites. Some are from later years when I got married and when we moved to the United States."

As Sara picked up each picture, she held them and smiled. Jill watched without saying anything more but watched Sara smiling.

She was wondering what was behind Sara's happy expression. As Sara picked up the picture of Jill and Enid, she thought back to the times her and Robert would go out for ice cream. She picked up the wedding photo and had a brief moment of sadness as she thought about her own eventual wedding, wishing that Robert could be there. The smile soon returned to her face as she thought to herself, *He will be there. He's always going to be there with me.*

Sara set the pictures down on the table and looked at Jill wide-eyed. "I have an idea of how we can write your story Jill. I'll be working on it." Jill smiled saying, "I know you'll do a great job, and thank you for helping me with a very difficult task. Let me know if I can help more."

As Sara rose from the table, she fought back the tears she knew were wanting to come. When she reached the door, she couldn't hold them back anymore. She turned to embrace Jill and began to cry while Jill hugged her tightly, saying nothing. When Sara finally let go, she turned without saying anything more and slowly walked to her car. Jill watched with tears in her own eyes, as Sara drove away.

'Sara thought of Robert the whole drive home. She so wished he was there to help her put Jill's story to paper. She smiled when she remembered her own, earlier thought that her brother would always be there with her. She was eager to get started telling the story of this very special lady.

Jill with Enid and her first ice cream cone

Jill and Enid in London

Jill and her brother Jack shortly after the war

Jill with brother Jack

Jill and her father earlier years in Guernsey

Baby Jill

Jills parents, Stanley and Olive Pay

Jill and her brothers, Jack, Roy, and Paul

Jill and Peter Oliver's wedding, pictured along with her father and mother, the   family doctor, Jill and Jack's nurse, and family friends.

Jill, Peter, and their children immigrating to the U.S. on the Queen Mary

Chapter 31:

It was four months later, and Sara was sitting at a table with her parents and Jill. They were in the Mershon Auditorium on the campus of Ohio State University in Columbus. Sara wasn't sure how many people were there, but it had to be hundreds. They had just enjoyed a wonderful steak dinner, followed by music performed by the Ohio State orchestra band. She felt more nervous than she had felt in a long time when a gentleman approached the podium up on the stage.

As the gentleman adjusted the microphone, the people in the audience began to quiet down. "I would like to welcome all of you once again to the 2022 Ohio High School History Essay celebration. We have had many awards presented already, but now is the time to introduce our 2022 First Place winner. Her essay on the true story of a woman, one who as a child spent three years in a German camp during World War II, was an excellent retelling of history. She told the story in a way that made one want to keep reading until the end. Ladies and gentlemen, will you please, give a huge Ohio State University welcome to the 2022 Ohio High School History essay winner, Sara Tessler."

People began clapping as Sara stood from her chair and started towards the stage. A young man held her hand and led her up the steps. As she reached the podium, the gentleman who had introduced her handed her a beautiful plaque and a large blue ribbon. He stepped back and held his arm out towards Sara as people continued clapping. Sara stood, just looking out at the crowd. She looked down at the table where her parents were sitting next to Jill. All three had huge smiles on their faces. Jill put her fingers to her lips to gesture a kiss towards Sara. Sara looked around the auditorium acknowledging the applause from everyone, when she stopped and stared toward the back of the auditorium. Standing against the wall was a handsome, athletic-looking young man. He gave her a wink, a big smile, and held two thumbs up…and then he was gone.

Epilogue

Jill Vincent Pay Oliver is a true-to-life, sweet, kind-hearted lady that lives in a lovely community in San Diego, California. She is in-fact that little girl more than 80 years ago that lived through all of the horrible experiences described in these pages. While Sara was a fictitious character, Jill Vincent Pay Oliver and her story are real. Jill and I continue to stay in contact. She is one of the most incredible and special people I have come to know. Life has been very good to Jill since those horrific years during World War II. Her father was able to rebuild his dental practice after they moved from Guernsey. After boarding school, Jill worked with her father at his dental practice, while continuing her education. Jill and her husband eventually immigrated to the United States, and she has called this country her home ever since. After completing her education, Jill began a career of teaching and helping students pass their exams for dentistry. Many of her students have kept in touch and have told her that they would not be where they are today if it had not been for her.

Jill has made several trips back to Guernsey over the years with friends and family members.

Guernsey still holds a special place in her heart despite those challenging times when she was a young girl.

I am honored to call her my friend, and so thankful that she trusted me to help tell her incredible story.

Acknowledgements

To my wife Kate Treadway, thank you for believing in me and encouraging me on this journey. I could not have done it without you by my side.

Thank you to Lissa Roberson for your help with the incredible job of editing you did.

A big thank you to Charmaine Morley for providing the digital copies of many of the pictures used.

Thank you to Cody Engdahl for all of your help in walking me through the publishing phase.

Of course, thank you Jill for your friendship and your trust in allowing me to help tell your incredible story.

For information contact David K. Treadway at

Dkt2u1@gmail.com 615-308-7129

408

Printed in Great Britain
by Amazon

24416246R00227